The Distinguishing Traits of Christian Character

By

Gardiner Spring
Pastor of the Brick Presbyterian Church
in the City of New York

Edited by
Dr. Don Kistler

The Northampton Press
. . . for instruction in righteousness. . .

The Northampton Press
A division of Don Kistler Ministries, Inc.
P.O. Box 781135, Orlando, FL 32878-1135
www.northamptonpress.org

ISBN 978-0-9798579-8-0

Library of Congress Cataloging-in-Publication Data

Spring, Gardiner, 1785-1873.
   [Essays on the distinguishing traits of Christian character]
   The distinguishing traits of Christian character / by Gardiner Spring ; edited by Don Kistler. – Northampton Press ed.
       p. cm.
   Originally published: Essays on the distinguishing traits of Christian character. New York : Dodge and Sayre, 1813.
   ISBN 978-0-9798579-8-0 (alk. paper)
   1. Christian life. I. Kistler, Don. II. Title.
   BV4501.3.S6645 2009
   248.4–dc22
                                                        2009036578

Contents

Introduction   v

Chapter 1   1
Visible Morality

Chapter 2   5
Form of Religion

Chapter 3   13
Speculative Knowledge

Chapter 4   16
Conviction of Sin

Chapter 5   28
Confidence in One's Good Estate

Chapter 6   42
Love for God

Chapter 7   56
Repentance

Chapter 8   66
Faith

Chapter 9   82
Humility

Chapter 10   92
Self-Denial

Chapter 11   102
A Spirit of Prayer

Chapter 12   110
Love for the Brethren

Chapter 13   115
Non-Conformity to the World

Chapter 14   123
Growth in Grace

Chapter 15   131
Practical Obedience

Chapter 16   140
Conclusion

Introduction

There is a hope that is as an anchor to the soul, and there is a hope that is as the spider's web. The former is built on the Rock of Ages, the latter on the sand. The one perishes when God takes away the soul; the other is sure and steadfast, entering into that which is within the veil.

The hope of the Christian is founded on evidence. The disciple of Jesus is ready to give an answer to every one who asks him a reason of the hope that is in him. He is born of the incorruptible seed. His hope does not make ashamed because the love of God is shed abroad in his heart by the Holy Ghost who is given unto him.

The hope of the self-deceived is founded on presumption. He is wrapped up in false security. A deceived heart has turned him aside. There is a lie in his right hand. He imagines he is right while he is fatally wrong; he hopes he is going to heaven while he is on the broad way to hell.

It is no inconsiderable thing, therefore, to possess the spirit of real religion. Multitudes substitute the shadow for the substance, and rest satisfied with a mere name to live. It is indeed no inconsiderable thing to have actually passed from death unto life. Multitudes cherish the hope of the divine favor who will at last be confounded with disappointment and sunk deep in despair. Let the reader, therefore, sit down to the following pages with this solemn question before him: Am I the friend of God, or am I His enemy?

It will be too late to put this question to you by and by. Perhaps you fear that you are God's enemy. Perhaps you hope that you are His friend. To aid you in deciding this interesting point is the design of the following pages. There are some things that are neither for nor against you; there are others that are decisively in your favor. The first five essays will exhibit several traits of character that cannot be relied on as conclusive evidence of genuine religion. The last ten will exhibit several that may be relied on without danger of deception.

The importance of the subject constrains the writer to use great freedom and plainness. The plainness that he has used also constrains him to beg his readers to suspend their decision of the solemn question before them until they shall have taken a full view of the subject. If anything should be said that wounds them, let them remember, it is the "wound of a friend." The honor of God, the value of the soul, and the awful retributions of eternity, all make me more solicitous to save you than to please you.

Searcher of hearts! Send out Thy light and Thy truth, and let them lead me. Discover their deception to the self-deceived, and make Thy dear children strong in the grace that is in Christ Jesus.

New York, October 5th, 1813

1

Visible Morality

"Man looketh on the outward appearance." It is not by a few that visible morality is viewed as the narrow way that leads to life. It would be an impeachment of the understanding of my readers to say that mere morality is not conclusive evidence of Christian character, were it not for the multitude of hopes that are built upon this crumbling basis. An unblemished moral character is in itself so amiable that it not only commands the respect and esteem of others, but secures the confidence of those who possess it. If a man is honest, industrious, and temperate, faithful to his promises, and punctual in his engagements; if he possesses a friendly, humane, kind, generous, and noble spirit, he views himself, and is viewed by the world around him, to be a "good-hearted man," and in a fair way to heaven! If he is correct in his external demeanor, if he avoids all overt acts of immorality, if he is innocent and harmless, if his honor is unsullied and his name without reproach, though he may confess that he is not so good as he should be, yet he believes he is much better than he is. He sees nothing to shake his hopes or alarm his fears. Look abroad into the world and see the thousands that rest here for eternity. Melancholy view! The heart is indeed deceitful above all things, as well as desperately wicked.

The man who is merely moral is a stranger to the living God. While he sustains an unimpeached character in the view of the world, he may neither believe the principles of the gospel

1

nor practice the duties of piety. He may be invincibly averse to every species of immorality on the one hand, but he is equally so to the exactness and spirituality of religion on the other. The infinitely important duties that he owes to God, he keeps entirely out of sight. Of loving and serving Him, he knows nothing. Whatever he does, or whatever he leaves undone, he does nothing for God. He may be honest in his dealings with everybody except God. He robs none but God. He is thankless and faithless to none but God. He speaks reproachfully of none but God. A just view of the relation that he bears to God forms no part of his principles, and the duties that result from that relation form no part of his morality. He contents himself with mere external conformity to the duties of the second table. Like the young man in the gospel, he may not have committed murder, nor adultery, nor theft, nor perjury, from his youth up, while, like him, he may have laid up treasures for himself and not be rich toward God. He is earthly and sensual rather than heavenly and spiritual.

In the sight of God, such a character is radically defective. The moral man is like Israel of old: an empty vine, because he brings forth fruit to himself. He is no better than the unprofitable servant; no better than a cumberer of the ground, who will at last be cut down and cast into the unquenchable flame.

Let it not be forgotten, however, that no man has the least claim to Christian character who is not what the world calls a moral man. Vital religion is an operative principle. The spirit of piety not only lives in the heart, but flows forth in the life. A good tree cannot bring forth evil fruit. Whatever may be the pretensions of an immoral man, he is far from the kingdom of heaven. Still, mere morality falls far short of the religion of the cross. The grand defect is, mere morality never aims at the heart, and would never touch it, if it should. The natural disposition may be very amiable, and the external demeanor very blameless, while the carnal heart is enmity against God.

The gospel of Jesus Christ requires men to be moral; and if this were all that it required, the moral man would be a Christian. But it requires them to be moral from holy principles. The gospel of Jesus Christ requires men to be honest, sober, industrious, and generous; but it requires them to be honest, sober, industrious, and generous from evangelical motives. "As a man thinketh in his heart, so is he." The moral quality of actions lies in the disposition of heart with which they are performed. A man may therefore be very honest, very humane, and very generous, but if the disposition of heart with which the acts of honesty, humanity, and liberality are performed, are not such as God requires and approves, he has no lot nor part in the portion of God's people.

There is a wide distinction between moral virtues and Christian graces. Christian graces spring from Christian motives, or such motives as are warranted by the gospel of Christ. They regard, in the first place, the glory of God and the interests of His kingdom, and then regulate our intercourse with our fellow men according to the principles of His Word. Moral virtues spring from selfish motives. They have no regard for the glory of God and the interests of His kingdom. They go just so far as self-interest leads the way, and there they stop. Such are the virtues of men dead in trespasses and sins; such is the morality of "philanthropists"; such is the morality of the heathen; such is the morality of infidels.

Reader, look into your Bible. Will such morality be of any avail in the solemn hour that tries the spirits of men? To the law and the testimony: Every page will flash conviction on the conscience that such spurious morality is of no account in the sight of God. I say, in the sight of God. The moral man has a higher claim upon the regard and confidence of his fellow men than the immoral man. He is a better ruler and a better subject, a better parent and a better child, a better master and a better servant, than the immoral man. Other things being equal, he is less guilty in the sight of God than the immoral man. But after all, he lacks the one thing needful. He is a child of wrath. He is without Christ, an alien from the commonwealth of Israel, a stranger from the covenants of promise; and though he may cherish a delusive hope, is without God in the world.

2

Form of Religion

"Many," says an old writer, "take the press-money and wear the livery of Christ who never stand to their colors nor follow their leader." The character of the formalist ranks higher in the estimation of the world than the character of the mere moralist. Formalists advance a step further than visible morality, and maintain the form of religion. They are those who are not only decent in their external deportment among men, but strict in the observance of all the duties of piety. They put on the appearance of real religion. But this is not conclusive evidence of their Christian character.

We read of those who have the form of godliness, but who deny the power thereof. Men may maintain the form of godliness from a variety of motives, none of which spring from the operation of grace in the heart. Many persons do it for the sake of reputation. A due regard for the institutions of Christianity forms so essential a part of the character of the good citizen that among a virtuous people it is difficult to secure esteem and confidence without a becoming observance of the external duties of religion. Such is the homage that vice pays to virtue that in Christian communities it is a creditable thing to put on the appearance of religion. To those who regard the good opinion of the world around them, there are not wanting multiplied motives to appear better than they really are.

No small portion of those who maintain the mere form of

religion do it from the force of education. A religious education cannot fail to have a desirable influence, in a greater or less degree, upon all, both in restraining them from the commission of crime and in impelling them to the external performance of duty. It often does have this influence upon many during the whole course of their lives. It is difficult to break over the restraints that have been imposed by parental instruction and example without singular boldness and the most brutish stupidity. Hence you find many who persevere in the usual forms of religion to the end of life who give you no satisfactory reason to believe that their hearts are right with God. The observance of the external services of piety has become a habit; and they walk the customary round of duties because it is a beaten path rather than because it is a pleasant one.

Perhaps a still greater number maintain the appearance of godliness for the sake of quieting the clamors of natural conscience. The inspiration of the Almighty has implanted a principle in the human breast that is capable of discerning the immutable difference between right and wrong, of giving men a sense of moral obligation, and of approving what is right and condemning what is wrong in their moral conduct. There are seasons when the silent voice of that invisible agent, who is commissioned by God to record the sins of thought and action, whispers that God is angry with the wicked every day. The implacable foe stings with anguish and convulses with agony. In these seasons of remorse, the carnal heart naturally flees to the covenant of works. When the moral principle is awake, there can be nothing that looks like a compromise between the heart and the conscience short of a life of external godliness. The conscience is so seriously affected with divine truth, as often and for a length of time, not to allow some of the worst of men in the omission of any of the external duties of religion.

There are also those who maintain the form of religion for the sake of fostering the persuasion of their own good estate. We know that "there is a way which seemeth right to a man, but the end thereof are the ways of death." Men who are experimentally ignorant of the nature of real religion easily substitute the shadow for the substance. Externally, the formalist does not differ from a real saint. He performs all those overt acts of religion that he would perform if he were at heart a sincere follower of Christ. Hence the beauty of his external conduct induces him to imagine that he is so. Thus Paul felt before the law of God came home to his conscience, discovered his guilt, and swept away his carnal hopes. And thus the foolish virgins felt till the midnight cry was given, "Behold, the Bridegroom cometh!" Rather than give up their hope, formalists continue to cherish their deception by substituting the appearance for the reality, till their deception, their hope, and their irksome forms vanish together, and leave them amid the wailings of the eternal pit.

There are very many who, from some one of these causes, or all of them combined, carry the form of godliness to every possible extent, and are still nothing more than sounding brass or a tinkling cymbal. This was eminently the character of the Pharisees. They were what their name denotes them to have been, separatists distinguished for their rigid manner of life and great pretensions to sanctity. They fasted often, made long prayers, paid tithes with exactness, and distributed alms with liberality. As a badge of distinction, they wore large rolls of parchment on their foreheads and wrists on which were inscribed certain words of the law. As an exhibition of their purity, they never entered their houses or sat down at their tables without washing their hands. They would not so much as touch a publican, or eat or drink or pray with a man who was a sinner. But all this was corrupted by an evil heart of unbelief, and served only to flatter their pride and fill up the measure of their iniquity. All this was consistent with shutting up the kingdom of heaven, and neither going in themselves nor suffering them who are entering to go in. All this was denounced by one woe after another, as the hypocrisy of men who should therefore receive the greater damnation.

We need not go far to look for multiplied testimony that there are those in this age of the church who, like the Pharisees, outwardly appear righteous unto men, but within are full of hypocrisy and iniquity. It is not difficult to make clean the outside of the cup and of the platter. Men may read and pray; they may attend to the duties of the family and the sanctuary, and often to those of the closet; they may profess to be on the Lord's side, give up their children to God in baptism, come themselves to the sacramental table, and engage in the solemn act of commemorating the love of the Lord Jesus—and yet know no more of real, vital piety than the prayerless and profane. Especially is this too often true of those who are baptized in their infancy, and educated under the care of those churches who admit them into their communion, for no other reason and with no other evidence of their good estate than that they have received the initiating seal of the church.

The lax practice of admission to sealing ordinances is an evil that cannot be too deeply deplored. In cities where there is unhappily something like the spirit of rivalry in the churches, it is one of the most dangerous snares of the fowler. Ministers and elders often yield to the temptation and, it is to be feared, receive many into the church who will at last be weighed in the balances, and found wanting.

The ordinance of the Lord's Supper is the peculiar privilege of believers.

In the act of commemorating the love of the Lord Jesus, there is a virtual, nay, there is an express profession of saving faith in the Lord Jesus. Now the Word of God justifies no man in professing to possess that which he does not possess. If it does, it warrants him in professing a lie. Those, therefore, who have a right to the ordinance of the Supper are real believers.

"This cup," said the ever-blessed Redeemer, "is the New Covenant in My blood." It is the seal of that covenant; none therefore have the warrant to partake of it except those who are within the pale of that covenant. Believers only are in that covenant; therefore, believers only have a right to its seal.

The cup of blessing that we bless, is it not the communion of the blood of Christ? The bread that we break, is it not the communion of the body of Christ? For we being many are one bread and one body; for we are all partakers of that one bread. This grand privilege that believers enjoy at the sacramental table, communion with Christ and with each other, rests upon the vital union of the soul to Christ by faith. Believers become members of His body. They have all drunk into one spirit, and are also all members one of another. None, therefore, have a right to come to the sacramental table who are not real believers; for no others have the spirit of communion with Christ and His disciples.

The right of access to the ordinance of the Supper, we know does not limit the right of admission. It is not our prerogative to judge the heart. After exercising all her wisdom, a church may admit some to her communion who ought not to be admitted and debar others who have a right to the privilege. Still, the right of admission is not independent of the right of access. Notwithstanding we cannot judge the heart, it is our indispensable duty to form our opinions and regulate our conduct from the best evidence that we can obtain. It is our indispensable duty to receive those who are, and to reject those who are not, in the judgment of Christian charity, real believers. To multiply communicants merely for the sake of multiplying them, to make converts faster than the Spirit of God makes them, to add to the church those whom the Lord does not add, gives her neither strength nor beauty. Better is it that the church should be a small, select band, cemented by ardent love to their Master and His interest, than a discordant multitude, without harmony of sentiment and affection. The three hundred that lapped under Gideon, the type of Christ, were more potent than the mighty host of Midian and Amalek. Union is the strength and beauty of our Zion. Union, not numbers, will make her terrible as an army with banners.

But their condemnation is as sure as their guilt is great. To look for conclusive evidence of Christian character in the mere form of Christianity is to expect the evidence of purity where there is nothing but the marks of pollution. The mere formalist is exceedingly sinful. No man has a right to be a formalist, whether his formality arises from hypocrisy or self-deception, or both. He has no right to deceive himself or to deceive others. Every species of mere formality is viewed by God as no better than detestable. How did He express his displeasure towards His ancient people for this sin? "This people," said He, "draweth nigh unto Me with their mouth, and honoreth Me with their lips, but their heart is far from Me." God also demands of His people, " 'To what purpose is the multitude of your sacrifices unto Me?' saith the Lord? When ye come to appear before Me, who hath required this at your hands to tread My courts? Bring no more vain oblations; incense is an abomination unto Me; the new moons and sabbaths, the calling of assemblies, I cannot away with. It is iniquity, even the solemn meeting.' " God sets the guilt of formalists in the most striking light by the words of the prophet: "He that killeth an ox is as if he slew a man; he that sacrificeth a lamb, as if he cut off a dog's neck; he that offereth an oblation, as if he offered swine's blood; he that burneth incense, as if he blessed an idol." Killing an ox in sacrifice was required, but killing a man was forbidden; sacrificing a lamb was required, but sacrificing a dog was forbidden: oblations were required, but swine's blood was forbidden; burning incense was required, but blessing or worshiping an idol forbidden. Hence, so far is the mere form of devotion from being either acceptable to God or evidence of our own good estate that it is no better than if we slew a man or worshiped an idol.

Be not deceived, for God is not mocked. All are not Israel that are of Israel. He is not a Jew who is one outwardly. There are many who are called by the name of Israel, who swear by the name of the Lord and make mention of the God of Israel, but not in truth, nor in righteousness. Like the Pharisees, you may pray long and fast often; and, like them, you may be a generation of vipers and never escape the damnation of hell.

> Their lifted eyes salute the skies,
> Their bended knees the ground;
> But God abhors the sacrifice,
> Where not the heart is found.

Oh, how often is this picture presented in real life! "God, I thank Thee that I am not as other men, or even as this publican." Would that you were more like him! Your corrupt heart corrupts all the fair forms of your devotion, and you are still in the gall of bitterness and the bonds of iniquity. The hope of formalists is the offspring of a deceived and a wicked heart. It is an affront to the majesty of heaven; it is a violation of the laws of His empire; it gives the lie to the Author of eternal truth. Hence the state of formalists is full of danger. They are singularly prone to cherish their deception. They are taken in their own craftiness. They flatter themselves in their own eyes till their iniquity is found to be hateful. They rest in a hope that will at last bite like a serpent and sting like an adder.

3

Speculative Knowledge

Speculative knowledge is no less deficient in the testimony that it bears to Christian character than visible morality or the form of religion. Neither is conclusive.

Speculative knowledge is by no means to be undervalued. Ignorance, in most cases, is far from being venial; error is always more or less sinful. It is of serious importance that the opinions of men be formed, and formed upon the principles of the unerring standard. There can be no spiritual knowledge where there is no speculative knowledge. God cannot be loved where He is not known. Truth is the natural aliment of all gracious affections. But though there can be no spiritual knowledge where there is no speculative knowledge, there may be much speculative knowledge where there is no spiritual knowledge. Though the want of speculative knowledge may be decisively against you, the possession of it is not necessarily in your favor.

We have only to open our eyes to discern the fact that very wicked men are sometimes orthodox in their sentiments. Wicked men, as well as good men, are endowed with perception, reason, and conscience. And they are as capable of applying these faculties in reflecting upon moral objects as upon natural objects. They are not only capable of understanding the truth, but often understand it with accuracy. How many have you seen who were thoroughly versed in the Scriptures, who had correct theoretical views of the character of God, the character of man, the character and offices of Christ, of the necessity,

13

nature, and cause of regeneration, who comprehended a connected system of theology and were distinguished champions for the faith; who were, notwithstanding all this, strangers to the religion of the heart! "Thou believest there is one God. Thou dost well. The devils also believe and tremble."

Satan himself was once an angel of light. There is no more studious observer of the character and designs of God than the great adversary of both. There is no greater proficient in theological truth than the father of lies. There is no want of orthodoxy even in hell.

For the existence of this fact we are not at a loss for satisfactory reasons. Speculative knowledge has its seat in the head, vital religion in the heart. There is no moral goodness in the simple assent of the understanding to truth. We receive, compound, and compare ideas whether we wish to or not. When we see the evidence of a proposition to be clear, we cannot withhold our assent to it while we may hate the truth we receive and love the error we reject. Besides, there is nothing in the nature of speculative knowledge to produce holy affection. The twilight of reason and conscience, and the clear sunshine of the gospel, are in themselves equally unadapted to the causation of holiness. All the light of eternity breaking in upon the understanding of the natural man cannot create one spark of holy love. You may follow the natural man through every possible degree of instruction; and though his head will be better, his heart will be worse. It is irrational to suppose that a clear view of an object that is hated will produce love to the object. If, when the character and truth of God are partially seen, they are the objects of hatred, when clearly seen they will become the objects of malignity. The understanding, therefore, may be enlightened while the heart remains perfectly vitiated.

Far be it from us by these remarks to exclude from our

theology the doctrine (
of this doctrine will g
between those who in
glorify Him as God. I
disposition, is changed :
illumination, the soul w
may be felt. The souls
remained without form
moral chaos merged in sh
God who commanded the
into their hearts to give th   glory
of God in the face of Jesus

This is a kind of knowledge, however, that is far above mere intellectual speculation. It is not immediately the object of intellectual speculation, but of gracious affections. This is a kind of knowledge that is both of divine origin and divine nature. This is the knowledge that edifies; all other puffs up. The essential difference between that knowledge which is, and that which is not conclusive evidence of Christian character, lies in this: The object of the one is the agreement of the several parts of a theological proposition; the object of the other is moral beauty, the intrinsic loveliness of God and divine things. The sinner sees and hates; the saint sees and loves. The prophecy of Isaiah is fulfilled in the experience of thousands: "Hearing they shall hear, and not understand; and seeing they shall see, and not perceive." Something more is necessary to make a man a Christian beside the enlightening of the natural understanding. Beware of the hope that is built on no firmer basis than a just speculative view of the doctrines of the gospel!

4
Conviction of Sin

It is not strange that natural men should sometimes be alarmed by a sense of their danger. When they see that the judgments that God has denounced against sin will sooner or later overtake them, that they are rapidly passing to the gates of death, and that they are unprepared for the solemn realities of the future world, it is impossible for them to remain unmoved. They begin to think seriously of the things that belong to their everlasting peace. They cease to make light of that which is important, and to view as important that which is lighter than vanity. They begin to see things as they are. The value of the soul, the indispensable necessity of an interest in the blood of sprinkling, heaven, and hell, these are subjects that engage their most serious reflection and excite the most fearful alarm. But, strange to tell, how soon does their solemnity vanish! How often is their alarm momentary! The lapse even of a few weeks may convince you that all this is but the early cloud and the morning dew, that quickly passes away.

A variety of considerations induce us to believe that no degree of conviction for sin is conclusive evidence of Christian character. The simple conviction that I am a sinner is common to all men. That view of sin that arises from its hateful nature, as committed against the Holy God, is peculiar to saints. There is a state of mind differing from both these, from the former in degree and from the latter in kind, which is designated by the phrase "conviction for sin."

Impenitent sinners are often brought to see their own

sinfulness. God gives them a just view of their character. They are favored with a discovery of the total corruption of their hearts. They see that they do not have the love of God in them. They are made sensible that they are under the dominion of the carnal mind that is enmity against God. The divine law, in all the reasonableness of its precept, and all the equity of its sanction, comes home to the conscience with power, and brings with it the knowledge of sin and the sense of guilt. They see its extent and spirituality as well as its righteousness. They feel as Paul felt: when the commandment came, sin revived and he died. Sin does actually revive. The law that binds their consciences excites the enmity of their hearts. The more clearly they discern its righteousness and spirituality, the more vigorously they hate its divine Author. They begin to learn what kind of hearts they cherish. They see that in them there dwells no good thing. In vain they search for the least holiness, or a single duty, in all that they have done. Every imagination of the thoughts of their hearts is only evil continually. All their words and all their actions, all their desires and all their prayers, are directly contrary to the holy law of God.

Now, permit me to ask, is there any religion in all this? There can be none surely in possessing a depraved heart; and there is none in merely being sensible that we possess it. In the simple discovery that I am an atrocious sinner there is no sense of the hateful nature of sin, no sorrow for sin, no desire to be delivered from its power. To see my aggravated sinfulness and not be humbled on account of it is evidence of unyielding enmity rather than cordial reconciliation. If a strong sense, or, if you please, the strongest sense of personal sinfulness, were conclusive evidence of personal religion, every reprobate at the bar of judgment, and all the damned in hell, would be Christians. A sense of their corruption forms no small part of their wretchedness. We know from the unequivocal declaration of eternal truth that when the Lord comes with ten thousand of His saints to execute judgment upon all, He will convince all who are ungodly among them of all their ungodly deeds that they have ungodly committed. How then can the conviction of ungodliness be the evidence of godliness?

In the minds of the unregenerate, the sense of personal sinfulness is always accompanied with the apprehension of danger. It cannot be otherwise. When a sense of sin is fastened upon the conscience of the sinner, it cannot fail to throw him into distress. In many cases, the distress is great. The "law work" is severe. The unhappy man sees the corruption of his own heart, and therefore gives up all hope from his own righteousness. He sees the corruption of his own heart, and therefore gives up all hope from the prospect of amendment. The law that he has broken sweeps away at a stroke all his righteousness, and cuts up his hopes, root and branch. All that is past is bad; all that is to come is no better. He sees that, with his present disposition, sin will only revive and increase every hour that he lives. He is wretched and forlorn. He knows that he is the prisoner of justice, and fears that he is already bound over to the curse. He looks around for help, but no kind arm will interpose. He ventures to make a struggle to shake off his bondage, but every effort evidences his weakness; every struggle binds him faster in his chains. The arrows of the Almighty are within him, the poison whereof drinks up his spirits. He sees that he is actually going to hell. He knows that nothing he shall ever do will prevent his going there. There is but a step between him and the eternal pit, while an invincibly obstinate heart cuts him off from every successful effort to escape it.

The inability of the natural man to repent and believe the gospel lies in a heart so corrupt that it is absolutely invincible except by the almighty power of God. It is an inability, the very essence of which consists in his moral turpitude. This the convinced sinner knows. He may not, in form, recognize the distinction between moral and natural inability, but every pang that shoots through his heart is decisive testimony of its correctness. With the deep sense that he is in danger is connected the deep conviction that he is without excuse. He no longer casts the blame on God. The door of hope is open. Every obstacle, except that which arises from his own aversion to the way of life, is removed. All things are ready; he alone is unwilling. While he beholds himself trembling upon the verge of the pit, and hears the voice of the Great Deliverer—"Sinner, lay down the weapons of your rebellion; repent of all your transgressions; come unto Me"—he will not come. At terms like these, every feeling of his heart revolts. Lay down the weapons of his rebellion! Repent of all his transgressions! Come unto Christ! He will not; he cannot. He spurns the offers of mercy, and would rather die than submit. Here is his inability, an inability that is all of his own cherishing, all confined within his own carnal heart.

It would be well if those who feel so uncharitably, and speak so unadvisedly concerning persons who are conscientiously constrained to maintain both the reality and importance of the distinction between natural and moral inability, understood either themselves, or the doctrine they condemn. In giving the sinner a natural power to become holy, we do not claim for him the self-determining power of the will. We do not say that he can produce holiness by an act of the will that is antecedent to the first exercise of holiness. Neither do we challenge for a worm of the dust the prerogative of independence. Eternal life hangs on the sovereign grace of God. The work of renewing and sanctifying the soul, and bearing it to heaven at last, rests on His almighty arm. In giving the sinner a natural power to become holy, we design to give God the throne and humble the sinner at His feet. Now until this important truth ceases to glorify God and abase His enemies, let it be denounced as a doctrine either replete with error or devoid of meaning.

Natural ability consists in possessing all those faculties that are necessary to constitute a moral agent. A moral agent is a being that is capable of actions that can be compared with law. To be capable of nothing that can be compared with a rule of action, commanding what is right and prohibiting what is wrong, is to be reduced to the level of the brutes that perish. To be capable of this is to possess understanding, conscience, will, and affections. These faculties of the mind constitute a moral agent, and make any being capable of choosing or refusing, acting right or wrong as he pleases. Destitute of these, he would not be capable of moral action. He could be neither holy nor sinful. His character and conduct could be neither worthy of praise nor blame. But, possessing these, he possesses all that is necessary to the exercise of holy and unholy affections. He possesses the power to perceive the objects of love and hatred, to feel the obligation of loving that which is right and hating that which is wrong, and to love or to hate in conformity with the dictates of his conscience and understanding, or in defiance to the dictates of both.

This is what we mean by natural ability to become holy. Take away these faculties and there is a natural inability. Take away these and it is absolutely impossible that anything in the form of merit or demerit should be attached to human character. This is the ability that we claim for the sinner. Strip him of those faculties that are necessary to the exercise of volition and you convert him to a mere animal. Invest the animal with these faculties and you convert him into a moral agent; you make him the subject of moral government, accountable for his conduct. There is a spirit in man, and the inspiration of the Almighty has given him understanding. The sinner's claim must be acknowledged. He has all the natural faculties that are necessary to holiness and, if he were disposed to use them aright, he would be holy. You say a man has power to see and hear if he has the faculties that are necessary to seeing and hearing. So has he power to be holy if he has the faculties that are necessary to holiness.

But while we say that the sinner is under no natural inability to become holy, we also say that he is under a moral inability to become holy.

When we speak of the moral inability of the sinner, we do not mean to deny that his inability is original, innate. We know it is. We use the word "moral," in contradistinction from natural, to denote that which is comparable with a rule of moral action. Thus we speak of moral and natural good, moral and natural evil. There is much natural good in a seasonable shower of rain, but there is no moral good. There is much natural evil in an earthquake, but there is no moral evil. Natural good and evil cannot be compared with a rule of action; they bear no relation to praise or blame. With moral good and evil it is otherwise. I hope to be understood therefore when I use the phrase "moral inability."

Moral inability is comparable with a rule of action; it is not that which bears no relation to praise or blame. It consists in the total depravity of the carnal heart. It consists in an aversion to holiness that cannot be overcome. You can conceive of a man's possessing a given degree of aversion to holiness. You can see that the difficulty of his becoming holy will rise in proportion to his aversion to holiness. If his aversion to holiness is inconsiderable, the difficulty of becoming holy will be inconsiderable. If his aversion to holiness is great, the difficulty of becoming holy will be great. Now the aversion of the natural man to holiness is not inconsiderable; it is not merely great; it is complete and entire; it pervades every thought, every affection, and every design. By the arm of flesh it is invincible. It is open to no successful attack. Light, motives, and means of whatever character are in themselves of no avail to remove it.

Here is an inability; here is a serious inability. It is an inability that belongs to every man who is dead in trespasses and sins. But it is a moral and not a natural inability. It is an inability that is capable of being compared with law, and therefore bears relation to praise and blame. It consists wholly in a deeply rooted aversion to all that is good. Take away this, and where is the obstacle in the way of the sinner's becoming holy? What becomes of his natural inability? Let those who affirm that there is an inability in the sinner to become holy, aside from this mere moral inability, go into their closets and ask themselves these two questions:

What other inability is there in the sinner to become holy than his invincible aversion to holiness?

What is the point of difference between the natural powers of the saint and the sinner?

When they have given fair, logical answers to these questions, they need not be disappointed if they find themselves driven to the result that the inability of the sinner to become holy is no other than a moral inability. By the work of regeneration, the saint receives no new natural faculty. Passing from death unto life is a moral, and not a physical change. The only point of difference between the power of the saint and the sinner is that the saint has moral ability to be holy; the sinner does not. The sinner cherishes a moral inability to become holy; the saint does not.

"But, after all," one might object, "an inability is an inability, whether it is moral or natural! You deny the sinner a self-determining power. You grant that he has no ability that can produce holiness by an act of the will that is antecedent to the exercise of holiness." Neither can saints.

"You grant that he cannot become holy without the special operations of the Holy Spirit." Neither would saints ever have another holy feeling without the special operations of the Holy Spirit.

"Still, an inability is an inability; and what profit is there in your boasted distinction?"

Much in every way: Chiefly because, without it, we cannot have just views of the character of God and the guilt of the sinner.

Of the character of God: God invites sinners to be holy. He expostulates with them. He entreats them. He commands them to be holy. He threatens them with eternal death, and executes the threatening to the uttermost, if they persist in the refusal to yield to His requisitions. Now if they are naturally unable to yield, they must lie down in everlasting sorrow for not doing that which in its own nature cannot be done. But, is this the God who reigns in heaven? Has He commanded men to perform impossibilities, and does He damn them because they cannot obey? Does He forever abandon them to darkness and despair for not becoming holy, while He has withheld the faculties that are necessary to the exercise of holiness? No, it cannot be! Will not the Judge of all the earth do right? What if God had suspended the eternal destiny of your immortal soul upon your going from New York to Rome in a day? What if He had commanded you to create a world? You would not hesitate to say that it is unjust. But He has required you to become holy. And you say that you have no more, and no other power to become holy, than you have to go from New York to Rome in a day, or to create a world. What then should make the one unjust and not the other?

But such is not the character of the Holy God. The doctrine of man's natural inability is a libel on His righteousness. On the other hand, if all the inability of the sinner consists in his aversion to holiness; if he is under no natural inability; if he has as much power to become holy as saints; and all his inability arises from invincible perverseness—then God will be glorious in sending him to hell. He ought to go there; and all heaven will say, "Amen! Alleluia!" while the smoke of his torments is ascending forever and ever. " 'Come now, and let us reason together,' saith the Lord. 'Are not My ways equal? Are not your ways unequal?' " There would be no ground for these expostulations upon the principle of man's natural inability.

Neither can we have just views of the guilt of the sinner without recognizing the distinction between natural and moral inability. It is one thing to feel wretched, another to feel guilty; it is one thing to feel that you are lost and ruined, another to feel that you have destroyed yourself; it us one thing to claim pity, another to deserve blame. Mere calamity is one thing, and moral turpitude is another. Speak of man's inability without making it his crime, and his conscience will love the opiate. Speak of it as consisting in the free, voluntary exercises of his corrupt heart, and you leave him without excuse. He will feel that if he dies eternally, he is the voluntary author of his own destruction. He will never feel to blame for not performing impossibilities.

Bring this question then before the Judgment Seat of Christ. Annihilate the natural ability of the sinner to repent and believe the gospel; and if you make God glorious in banishing the impenitent to hell, and the impenitent deserving of their doom, the controversy is at an end. Until then, we must be allowed to speak on God's behalf; we must ascribe righteousness to our Maker.

Man is beyond the reach of help on this side of heaven. No means, no motives can afford him relief. He sees that he is in the hands of a sovereign God, and that everything without him, and everything within him, is conspiring to increase his guilt and aggravate his condemnation. And you will now ask, "Is there no religion in this?" None. Does vital religion consist in the apprehension of danger, or in the fear that we shall never escape it? Where is the holiness of being afraid of hell? What Christ-like affection is there either in the horror of a guilty conscience or the anticipation of the wrath to come?

"These are feelings that," as the learned Dr. [John] Owen well remarked, "do not belong to the precept of the law, but to its curse; they are no part of what it requires, but of what it inflicts."

In the mind of a convinced sinner, the sense of personal sinfulness is also connected with the sense of ill desert. When a man has a clear view of his own sinfulness, he not only sees that he is exposed to the wrath of God, but that he is *justly* exposed to the wrath of God. He sees that he deserves the displeasure of the Almighty throughout interminable ages. He is stripped of all his thin excuses, and is sensible that his sins are wholly unjustifiable. As he has before been constrained to acknowledge the reasonableness of the precept of the divine law, now he is constrained to admit the justice of its penalty. He has voluntarily and perseveringly disobeyed a law that is perfectly holy in itself, and clothed with the authority of the holy God; and he knows that it would be just if the penalty should be executed upon him to the uttermost. He knows that the holy God whose character he regards with enmity, whose law he transgresses with impenitence, whose gospel he rejects with disdain, can be under no obligation to save a wretch like him. And you will ask again, "Is there no religion in this?" Again I answer, and the reply is bottomed upon the word of eternal truth—not a whit! Is this no evidence that I have passed from death unto life? I answer, it is not conclusive evidence; and if this is all that you have experienced, it is none at all. If you are not sensible that you are so vile as to deserve the everlasting displeasure of God, you are not even a convinced sinner; but if you are sensible of this, you may not be a converted sinner. Vital religion does not consist in the approbation of the conscience to the condemning sentence of the law. Does not the conscience of every sinner, whether renewed or unrenewed, tell him that God would be just in abandoning him to misery without measure and without end? Do not the damned in hell feel that they are justly condemned? Was not the man without the wedding garment speechless? Will not the whole world become guilty before God at the last day?

If the view that I have given of this solemn subject will bear the test of God's Word, then the reader has a right to the plain result that no degree of conviction for sin is conclusive evidence of Christian character. Look at the feelings of a convinced sinner, and find, if you can, one spark of genuine holiness. Find, if you can, one Christian grace. Find, if you can, anything more than all those have felt who have gone down to the pit in their blood.

But may not these be the feelings of real Christians? I answer, they may be; but they are not the feelings that constitute the essential difference between real Christians and impenitent sinners. All who have passed from death unto life have, in a greater or lesser degree, been convinced of their total corruption, alarmed at their danger, and made to acknowledge the justice of God in the penalty of His law. Indeed, it may be said that the greater part of real Christians have never been the subjects of conviction in the degree that has been here exhibited. Still, every Christian has experienced some of it; every Christian has felt the same conviction in kind. If, therefore, you are without anything like this conviction, you may be sure that you are without religion. Still, it does not follow that because you have this conviction you therefore have real religion. It is true that in the course of God's providence conviction always precedes conversion; but it is not always true that conversion follows conviction. There is no necessary connection between conviction and conversion. A sense of sin and danger does not slay the enmity of the heart. The conscience may be convinced while the heart is not renewed. The carnal mind not only may but does hate what the awakened conscience approves. It is no certain evidence that, because the conscience feels the weight of sin, the heart is humbled on account of it; that because the conscience approves of the rectitude of divine justice the heart bows to the divine sovereignty. The most powerful conviction of sin, therefore, is not conclusive evidence of Christian character.

5

Confidence in One's
Good Estate

It is easy for a hypocrite to deceive himself with false hopes and carnal presumptions. You may be strongly persuaded that you are a Christian; but this persuasion does not make you so. You may cherish the most unwavering confidence of your personal interest in the great salvation while you have no part nor lot in this matter.

The confidence of a man's own good estate is attained in different ways. Both the confidence itself and the mode of attaining it are often scriptural. A man may be persuaded that he is a Christian because he has reason to believe that he possesses the Spirit of Christ. "Hereby know we that we dwell in Him, and He in us, because He hath given us of His Spirit." A man may be persuaded that he is a child of God because he discerns in himself those graces that are peculiar to the childlike character. He may have received the Spirit of adoption, whereby he cries, "Abba, Father." "The Spirit itself," said the apostle, "beareth witness with our spirit that we are the children of God."

A persuasion arising from such evidence is well-grounded. Such a persuasion cannot be too confident. It not only may but ought to rise to the full assurance of hope. It did in Job. "I know," said he, "that my Redeemer liveth; and though after my skin worms destroy this body, yet in my flesh shall I see God;

whom I shall see for myself, and mine eyes shall behold, and not another." It did in David: "As for me, I will behold Thy face in righteousness; I shall be satisfied when I awake in Thy likeness." It did in Asaph: "Thou shall guide me with Thy counsel, and afterwards receive me to glory." It did in the Apostle Paul: "I AM PERSUADED that neither death, nor life, nor angels, nor principalities, nor powers, nor things present, nor things to come, nor height, nor depth, nor any other creature, shall be able to separate us from the love of God, which is in Christ Jesus our Lord."

The comfortable assurance of believers enables them both to glorify and enjoy the ever-blessed God. It is as honorable to God to trust in His grace as to submit to His authority. When the hopes of believers are low and languishing, they do not know how deep the shade is they cast on the luster of divine forgiveness, how much they detract from the glory of the cross. The want of a cheerful hope, a humble reliance on the mercy of God, cannot fail to unman the most unwavering firmness and unnerve the most vigorous exertion. For those who have the witness of their good estate within them to sink down into a state of darkness that ends in the gloom of solitude and inactivity is sin. Many a good man, by having unhappily imbibed mistaken views of this subject, has rendered himself a mere cypher in the church, and a stumbling block to those who are out of it. Real Christians need not be afraid to cherish the full assurance of hope. There is something wrong in the state of that soul that refuses to be comforted. It is the duty of believers to make their calling and election sure. Assurance ought always to exist, and to be supported by corresponding testimony.

But this is not the vain confidence to which I allude in this essay. It bears no alliance to the presumption of the hypocrite and the self-deceived. There is a confidence that is obtained without the aid of God's Spirit, and cherished without the evidence of His Word.

Some rest this presumption on an unwarrantable notion that they entertain of the mercy of God. They are in the habit of viewing it as a general, indefinite, undistinguishing attribute. They imagine that because God is declared to be no respecter of persons, He exercises His mercy indiscriminately. They view Him as a being so fondly attached to the interest of His creatures as to pardon them without reference to the terms of the gospel, and save them without regard either to their own moral character, to the honor of His law, or to the well-being of His kingdom. They rely on no promise; they rest on no covenant. They are satisfied with the thought that God is merciful! They rest on the phantom, "uncovenanted mercy." Tell them that they are sinners, and they tell you that God is not strict to mark iniquity. Tell them that they have incurred the penalty of a righteous law and deserve to die, and they tell you that they have never done any harm; and, if they have, a merciful God will forgive them. God is too good to send them to hell! It cannot be that He will cast them off forever!

This is the subterfuge of thousands, the miserable hiding place that must be overflown when the billows of divine wrath beat upon this falling world. It is the fatal rock on which thousands have split. How many impenitent, Christ-less sinners have rested here for eternity! How many have I seen on a dying bed who did not have a spark of vital religion, who still indulged the hope that God was too merciful to damn them! My heart bleeds when I think of it.

Why do men forget that God is as just and as holy as He is gracious? All His perfections must be glorified. We cannot be saved at the expense of one of them. God regards His own glory and the interests of His kingdom more than everything else. To these everything must bow. If He were not too holy, too just, nay, too good to admit a totally depraved being into His kingdom, that kingdom would fall. Unholy men must be excluded from heaven because they are not fit for it. To exclude them is a part of that benevolent design, which is to make, on the whole, the most happy universe. God has the same benevolent motive for excluding the unholy from the heavenly state that He has for admitting the holy.

Yes, I do not hesitate to say that the benevolent God is too good to admit one unsanctified soul into the pure regions of the blessed. He has too great a regard for the honor of His character and for the excellence of His law. He loves the angelic host too well. He loves his people, He loves His Son too well ever to permit the song of the redeemed to feel the jar of one unhallowed tongue. The very thought is reproachful to his glory. No sin is there. The light of heaven shall never be darkened, even by the shadow of death. The designs of infinite benevolence shall never be frustrated by the introduction of one unholy being into the kingdom of God. Where, oh, where is the delusion of the miserable self-deceiver when justice exacts the uttermost farthing!

Others attain this persuasion in a manner still different. They have been taught that mere reformation and morality will not save them; and they are equally convinced that the form of religion will not save them. They see the necessity of possessing the real spirit of religion; and they begin to seek after it till they are weary of the search. They become awakened to a sense of their danger, convinced of their ill desert, and are thrown into some distress. But at length, through the influence of their own imaginations or the artful devices of the old serpent, they are inspired with hope and filled with joy. Some enrapturing vision has discovered to their view the Savior extended on the cross.

Some fancied messenger has announced that their sins are forgiven, and that God is their reconciled Father. Some text of Scripture, unsought, unexpected, and fatally misapplied, has whispered peace to the troubled conscience, and their souls are filled with raptures of joy. They imagine themselves almost ravished with a view of Christ's unutterable love, and with a view of it to them in particular.

They begin to mourn and lament over their sins, though not after a godly sort. They feel a kind of spurious sorrow, that they have ever hated so gracious and merciful a being as God. They have been abandoned to the delusion that their opposition to so kind and gracious a Being has been owing to some misapprehension of His character. Once they viewed Him as an "absolute God," as a God who was angry with the wicked, and angry with them. They viewed Him as their enemy, and dreaded the tokens of His displeasure.

But now they view His character in altogether a different light. They see that God is love. They are persuaded that He loves them. They are persuaded that He has pardoned their sins, and that it is His good pleasure to give them the kingdom. Now all their enmity is slain. They feel reconciled to God because they believe God is reconciled to them. Under the influence of this pleasing deception, they now begin to be happy. Religion absorbs all their attention; and the religion of the heart is what they think they admire and love. They are full of gratitude, full of peace and joy in believing that Christ died for them in particular. This persuasion of Christ's love for them now constrains them, and they imagine that they glory in nothing save the cross of Christ. They think they are ready to do anything, and to suffer anything for Christ's sake. The spirit of delusion runs high. They manifest for a while the greatest apparent zeal and engagedness. They cannot but glory in Him who has died for them, and who will finally advance them to endless blessedness in the kingdom of His Father.

All this is rotten at the core. However closely it may resemble the holy gratitude of God's people, it is but the counterfeit of that heavenly grace. It is purely selfish. It is mere mercenary religion. The Spirit of God has nothing to do with the root of it, nor the law of God with its fruits. There is not perhaps any error more common and more fatal among the serious part of mankind than this. This is the very religion that is agreeable to the feelings of the carnal heart. This was the religion of the impenitent Israelites. At the time of their deliverance from the house of bondage, and in view of the miracles both of mercy and judgment that had been wrought in their behalf, they sang the memorable "Song of Moses" on the banks of the Red Sea. But how soon do you find them murmuring at the waters of Meribah, and in the wilderness of Sin! The same scene, only in more awful colors, was again exhibited at the foot of Sinai. God appeared in all the greatness of His majesty. And when the people saw the thunderings, the lightning, the noise of the trumpet, and the mountain smoking, they removed and stood afar off. And they said unto Moses, "Speak thou with us, and we will hear; but let not God speak with us lest we die." Sad reversal! Scarcely forty days had elapsed than the very land that just beheld Jehovah descending in the cloud, and that trembled at the voice of His thunder, saw the golden calf, an idol, and heard the heathenish acclamation: "These be thy gods, O Israel, that brought thee up out of the land of Egypt!"

The same scene, though in more awful colors still, was exhibited in the streets of Jerusalem. No sooner did the Jews behold the miracles, and share in the favor of the promised Messiah, than they overlooked all the humbling circumstances of His birth and were anxious to make him their king. They followed Him with "hosannas," were impatient to see Him enrobed with the badges of royalty, and seated upon the throne of David, His father. But their attachment was soon put to a test that discovered its selfishness. They early found that the kingdom of the Messiah was a spiritual and not a temporal kingdom. They soon learned that he was not a Jew who was one outwardly; and that if they would be the subjects of his kingdom, they must become new creatures; must relinquish their attachment to the world; must deny themselves and take up the cross; must become holy in heart and in life, not too proud to relish the humbling religion of a crucified Savior, nor too righteous to submit to the righteousness of God.

Their hopes of individual grandeur and national glory, therefore, withered in the bloom. The promised Messiah became the object of neglect and malignity. No longer did they follow Him with acclamations of praise, but with the hiss of derision and the finger of scorn. No longer did their zeal prompt the cry, "Hosanna to the Son of David!" but their disappointed and infuriate selfishness instigated the malignant shout, "Crucify, Crucify!" Such is the religion of sinners. "Sinners," said the Savior, "love those who love them. Ye seek Me not because ye saw the miracles, but because ye did eat of the loaves, and were filled."

Far be it from me to say or to believe that all those who inculcate this kind of religion are to be ranked among the hypocrites and the self-deceived. We believe many of them to be Christians. The religion that they possess is better than that which they teach. Still, I do not hesitate to say that those who have no other religion have none at all that will stand the ordeal of the Last Day. A deceived heart has turned them aside.

On what is such religion founded? There is no supreme

attachment to the excellence of the divine character, to the holiness of the divine law, or to the perfection of the divine government. There is no supreme delight in the glory of the gospel for its own inherent excellence. On what then is such religion founded? Simply on the assumption, equally dishonorable to God and destructive to the souls of men, that there is, and there can be no loveliness in the divine nature, no glory in the divine perfections, but what results from God's particular love to them, and His designs to save them. A principle so reproachful to the character of the Deity, so reproachful to the cross of Christ, and so destructive to the souls of men has made many a man an enthusiast and a hypocrite, but never yet made one a humble follower of the Lord Jesus Christ. After all the glosses that can be put upon it, the amount of this principle is just this: Assure me of my salvation and the God of heaven is amiable and glorious; deprive me of my salvation and He is stripped of His loveliness and disrobed of His glory! Reader, does this look like taking your place in the dust and exalting God on the throne? Is this being reconciled to the character of God, or being supremely in love with yourself?

Though selfish piety is naturally blind to its own nature, yet the effect of this mercenary scheme is unequivocal. The grand sentiment of the system is that it is a mark of genuine holiness to be very anxious about your own welfare, but to care very little for the honor and glory of God. It is therefore a system that is perfectly compatible with supreme selfishness and, therefore, perfectly compatible with total depravity. There is nothing in all this with which the carnal mind is at enmity. If vital godliness consists in such a system of views and feelings, there is no need of a radical change of heart. Let the worst sinner on earth be persuaded that God loved him with an everlasting love, and from eternity designed to make him an heir of the heavenly inheritance, and his enmity will subside without any change of nature any alteration in the moral disposition of the soul.

The presumption on which we have been animadverting is one which any unrenewed man may cherish who is under the delusion of Satan and his own wicked heart. It is easy to say, "Pardon is mine; grace is mine; Christ and all His blessings are mine. God has freely loved me; Christ has graciously died for me; and the Holy Ghost will assuredly sanctify me in the belief, the appropriating belief, of these precious truths." It is no Herculean task for a heated imagination and an unsanctified heart to make these discoveries. This is a kind of confidence that the subtle Deceiver is interested to flatter and strengthen, till the unhappy subject has lost his hold and the Roaring Lion is sure of his prey. And the joys and sorrows, the zeal and engagedness, that spring from this delusion form a kind of religion that the blindness and deceit, the self-flattery and the pride of the carnal heart, very easily substitute for vital godliness.

Others attain the confidence of their own good estate in a manner still different. This mode of attainment is purely mechanical. According to the views of those who maintain this confidence, it seems to be "a strange kind of assurance, far different from other ordinary kinds; we are constrained to believe other things on the clear evidence that they are true, and would remain true, whether we believe them or not. But here our assurance is not impressed on our thoughts by any evidence of the thing; but we must work it out in ourselves, by the assistance of the Spirit of God." The very existence of this persuasion seems to be evidence of the truth of it. The proposition to be believed, that God freely gives Christ and His salvation to us in particular, is not true before we believe it, but becomes a certain truth when we believe it" (Walter Marshall,

The Gospel Mystery of Sanctification).

The amount of this is that a persuasion of your own personal interest in the blessings of the great salvation constitutes the essence of evangelical faith. If you can only believe that you will be saved, you are a believer, in the gospel sense of the word: Should you find any difficulty in doing this, you must work it out in yourselves by the assistance of the Spirit of God; and according to your faith so shall it be unto you. The persuasion, therefore, that you are a Christian makes you so; and the confidence that you will be saved renders your calling and election sure.

It is hardly necessary to guard the mind against the influence of this delusion. Reflecting men will not rest the hope of immortality on so treacherous a foundation unless they deliberately prefer the dreams of the self-deceived to the sober expectations of the real Christian. If there were no difference between being actually interested in the covenant of grace and the persuasion of our own minds that we are thus interested, this scheme might be plausible. Men must be Christians before they can be rationally persuaded that they are Christians. They must be the children of God before they can rationally cherish the confidence that they are so. It is not impossible, nor is it an unusual thing, for a man to be a Christian, and yet not to believe that he is a Christian. Nor is it less impossible and unusual for a man to believe that he is a Christian and yet not be a Christian. It is to be feared that there will be many at the Last Day who will say, "Lord, Lord!" unto whom the Bridegroom will say, "I never knew you; depart from Me, all ye workers of iniquity." There will be many in that day who have confidently believed that God freely gave Christ and His salvation to them in particular who will not find that it became a certain truth when they believed it. The error is too palpable to be ensnaring.

"When we affirm," said the eloquent [Joseph] Saurin, "that there is such a blessing as assurance of salvation, we do not mean that assurance is a duty imposed on all mankind, so that everyone, in whatever state he may be, ought to be fully persuaded of his salvation, and by this persuasion to begin his Christianity."

Let not the import of these remarks be misunderstood. Far be it from me to discourage the followers of the Lord Jesus from placing the most implicit reliance on the Author and Finisher of their faith. Every attribute of His character demands the most prompt and unreserved confidence. But, reader, real confidence in God is a thing widely different from a firm persuasion of your personal interest in His mercy. The former is your duty at all times. The latter is your duty, in the same proportion in which you have evidence that the love of God is shed abroad in your heart by the Holy Ghost. You have just as much evidence that you are interested in His pardoning mercy as you have that you are the subject of His sanctifying grace. Sanctification is the only evidence of conversion. The assurance of our acceptance with God depends on the assurance of our possessing the character of those who are accepted. The scriptural mode of obtaining assurance is that one pointed out by the Apostle Peter: "Giving all diligence, add to your faith, virtue; and to virtue, knowledge; and to knowledge, temperance; and to temperance, patience; and to patience, godliness; and to godliness, brotherly kindness; and to brotherly kindness, charity. For if these things be in you and abound, they make you that ye shall neither be barren nor unfruitful in the knowledge of our Lord Jesus Christ. Wherefore, brethren, give diligence to make your calling and election sure; for if ye do these things, ye shall never fall."

"The infallible assurance of faith," says our excellent

Confession of Faith of the Presbyterian Church, "is founded upon the divine truth of the promises of salvation, the inward evidence of those graces unto which these promises are made, the testimony of the Spirit of adoption witnessing with our spirits that we are the children of God; which Spirit is the earnest of our inheritance, whereby we are sealed to the day of redemption." To cherish the confidence of your own good estate when your graces are low and languishing, and while you live in the habits of sin, savors more of presumption than of humility. No man ought to live without some doubts of his own good estate who does not cherish such an abiding sense of divine truth, and live in such prevailing exercise of divine grace as to have the witness within him that he is born of God. It is in the exercise of grace alone that anyone ought to expect or even desire to find evidence of his being accepted in the Beloved. The evidence of our good estate rises in proportion to our love, to our repentance, to our humility, to our faith, to our self-denial, to our delight in duty. Other evidence than this the Bible does not know, and God has not given.

Let the reader beware of these vain confidences! When men rest satisfied with these presumptions, they usually rest satisfied until it is too late to be dissatisfied. They see nothing either within or without to shake their hopes or alarm their fears. Notwithstanding there is a wide and essential difference between these unscriptural confidences and the faith of the gospel; notwithstanding they have all the necessary means to know their true character, and could not mistake it if they would examine impartially—yet they sport themselves with their own deceivings, and do not know what manner of persons they are. You may easily imagine that you are safe; and, while the deception lasts, it may quiet your consciences and administer a short-lived consolation. But when the veil is drawn aside, when the dreams of time give way to the realities of eternity, these pleasing deceptions will vanish. There is less of this vain presumption in the hour of death than in the season of health and cheerfulness. There will be none of it at the left hand of the Judge; there will be none of it in hell.

The reader has now before him what the author designed to say in the first five essays. How solemnly these things call upon everyone to see whether his heart is right with God! If vital religion does not consist in visible morality; if it does not consist in the form of religion, nor in speculative knowledge, nor in mere conviction for sin, nor in the confidence of your own good estate, nor in the whole routine of enthusiastic experiences which that confidence inspires, nor in all these things combined—is it not time to look about you? In all that has hitherto been brought into view, there is not one holy exercise of heart, not one feeling that is in the least at war with supreme selfishness. There is not one fact, therefore, upon which I dare tell you that you may rely for eternity as conclusive evidence of Christian character.

How many are there who are almost Christians! As then you review the preceding pages, look with ingenuousness into your own heart. Men may think they are Christians, and yet be in the gall of bitterness and the bonds of iniquity. You may be almost saved and yet perish. You may get very near to heaven and yet go to hell. You may advance to the very verge of the better world and, from the threshold of glory, fall into the regions of mourning.

It may be that remarks like these will wound some of the dear children of God, while they leave the stupid hypocrite wrapped up in false security and impenetrable by nothing but the arrows of the Eternal. If the humble child of Jesus is hereby involved in darkness for a moment, his light shall soon break forth as the morning. If for a moment his strength and courage languish, they shall spring forth speedily; his righteousness shall go before him, and the glory of the Lord shall be his reward. The hypocrite will, in all probability, still cherish his deception; he will rest in carnal security till the awful moment when he lies gasping in the arms of death, and is just about to take his flight to the judgment seat of Christ. Then his refuges of lies shall be swept away, and his fancied security will only serve to render him the fairer mark of divine vengeance. Then he will discover his fatal mistake. Then his heart will tremble. Then his hopes will die within him. That which has been hidden shall be made known. The mask will be torn off; the secrets of the heart shall be unfolded; nothing shall remain unveiled. There will be no darkness or shadow of death, where the workers of iniquity may hide themselves. The sinners in Zion shall be afraid; fearfulness shall surprise the hypocrites: "Who among us shall dwell with devouring fire? Who among us shall dwell with everlasting burnings?"

6

Love for God

In the preceding chapters I have exhibited, as I proposed, a variety of views, feelings, and practices that cannot be relied on with safety as conclusive evidence of Christian character. In the subsequent ones, I propose to give a brief view of those that may be relied on without the danger of deception.

It is the excellence of the Christian religion that it makes a claim upon the affections. "My son, give me thine heart." "Love is the fulfilling of the law." "Though I give all my goods to feed the poor and give my body to be burned, and have not love, it profiteth me nothing."

At first view, there appears to be some difficulty in understanding with clearness what it is to love God. Men are in the habit of placing their affections upon beings that are the objects of sense. God is invisible. To profess to love a being that is not perceptible to our senses appears to some to savor more of the ignorance and wildness of enthusiasm than of the sober deductions of enlightened and sanctified reason. But though no eye has seen or can see the infinite and eternal Spirit, yet He has not left Himself without witness. There is a power in the human mind that enables it to form just notions of persons and things that cannot be perceived by sense. We need no other method of ascertaining the nature of love for God than the nature of love for man. The mode of reflection is in both cases the same. The process of compounding, comparing, and abstracting is the same. Seriously considered, there is precisely the same difficulty in conceiving of the nature of love for man that there is in conceiving of the nature of love for God. You know what it is to love your friend. And yet it is not the mere external form, it is not the animal, unanimated by the living, acting spirit that you love. But this is all that is perceptible to your senses. You see the motion, you hear the voice of your friend; and from the nature of what you see and hear you form the idea of his character. The soul, that which is characteristic both of the man and the friend, is invisible. What you see and hear is not that which you love, though it discovers to you something that is lovely. That which is the object of your senses suggests the existence and character of that invisible, thinking being which is the object of your affections, and which you either love or hate, as it pleases or displeases you.

You may as easily know what it is to love God, therefore, as you may know what it is to love your friend. The sensible signs by which He has communicated, and is every hour communicating His character, are vastly more significant than those which manifest the character of any other being in the universe. God is everywhere. The infinite Mind is ever active. It is the great Agent throughout all worlds. "The heavens declare the glory of God, and the firmament showeth His handiwork. Day unto day uttereth speech, and night unto night showeth knowledge. There is no speech nor language where their voice is not heard. Their line is gone out throughout all the earth, and their words to the end of the world." God has expressed His divine excellence in the work of His hands, and has exhibited the luster of His glory in the Word of His truth. Every act that He has performed, together with every word that He has spoken, is an unequivocal declaration of His character. It is easy to conceive that this character must be loved or hated, and that the invisible Being which this character unfolds must be the object either of complacency or aversion, of benevolence or malignity.

Love for God involves complacency in His character, benevolence toward His interest, and gratitude for His favors.

It involves complacency in His character. You see something in the character of your friend that to you appears pleasing and amiable. You see something that is lovely; and this loveliness is the foundation of your attachment. Thus the excellence of God is the foundation of all holy love. True love for God is a firm and steady principle that draws its motive and its sanction from His own intrinsic loveliness. It is delight in His excellence. Those who have put on the new man, which after God is created in righteousness and true holiness, love God because He is just such a God as He is; because His power is irresistible, His wisdom unerring, His purity spotless, His justice inflexible, His goodness universal, His grace infinite, and His designs eternal and immutable. Here holy love begins.

Wicked men are apt to consider God altogether such a one as themselves. They clothe the Divine Being with such attributes, and such only, as suit their depraved taste; and then it is no difficult thing to fall down and worship Him. But it is not God whom they worship; it is not God whom they love. It is an image that bears no resemblance to that glorious Being whom all heaven adores; it is a mere idol of their own imagination. Genuine complacency in God, therefore, is delight in His true character. The love that arises from delight in the character of a false god is enmity toward the true God. The enemies of God may love Him for what they imagine Him to be; none but the real friends of God love Him for what He is.

Supreme attachment to the character of God for His own inherent excellence draws the line of distinction between that love which is merely mercenary and that which is disinterested.

A man may be supremely selfish in the exercise of a certain kind of love for God. In all his love, he may have no ultimate regard except to his own happiness. He may delight in God for what He is to him, while he takes no delight in Him for what He is in Himself. Such is not the love of the newborn soul. The enmity of his heart toward God is slain. He is reconciled to the divine character as it is. God is the object of delightful contemplation to his devout mind. In his most favored hours, his views are diverted from himself. As his eye glances at the varied excellence of the deity, he does not stop to ask the question whether God is a being who will at all events regard his interest; it is enough for him that He will at all events regard His own glory. He beholds a dignity, a beauty in the divine character, that fills his soul with high devotion. All things else are atoms, motes, dust, and vanity. The feelings of the prophet are his: "The desire of my soul is to Thy name, and to the remembrance of Thee." The unchangeableness of the divine Being, and the perfections of the divine nature excite the noblest views and the most raised affections. The language of the Psalmist is his: "Whom have I in heaven but Thee? And there is none on earth that I desire beside Thee!" The soul is satisfied with God's perfect excellence, and does not cherish a wish that He should be different from what He is.

True love for God also implies benevolence toward Him, and the interest of His kingdom. In the intrinsic excellence of His character, God is the same yesterday, today, and forever. The fullness of perfection is equally necessary at all times to His very existence as God. It would, therefore, be arrogance in the worms of the dust to imagine that they may be profitable to God, as he who is wise may be profitable to himself; but it is presumption for them to imagine that they love Him without feeling a friendly interest in His designs, a sincere desire for the advancement of His cause, and the glory of His name. Those who love the divine character necessarily desire to promote the divine glory. They regard the honor of God as comprehending every good, and as concentrating every wish. In this, every holy mind takes supreme delight. It is the ardent desire, the highest wish of a sanctified heart, that in all his works, in all his plans, by all in heaven, by all on earth, and all in hell, God should be glorified. Those who have tasted and seen that the Lord is good have found unspeakable pleasure in beholding His glory, and therefore sincerely and ardently desire to behold greater and brighter displays of it. This sublime spirit enters into the essence of all genuine love for God. The infinite Being, who is capable of enjoying an infinitely higher degree of happiness than all created intelligence beside, shares largely in the benevolent affections of every devout mind.

Genuine love also involves the exercise of gratitude. Gratitude to God is the exercise of love for Him for the favors that He has communicated to us. The primary ground of love for God is the intrinsic excellence of His own character without regard to any personal interest in His favor. The first exercise of love for God is, and must be, antecedent to the persuasion that God loves us. Still, it is true that no man who loves God for the amiableness of His own character can refrain from loving Him for the favors that He has communicated to him in particular. The discovery of his personal interest in the favor that God bears to His own people will excite the most tender and grateful emotions. He cannot contemplate the care that has sustained him from year to year, the goodness that encircles him every hour that he lives, the Word that instructs him, and the discipline that is preparing him for better enjoyments, without some sensations of thankfulness. He cannot call to mind the promises that have supported him, the threats that have warned him, and the wonderful grace that has redeemed him without admiration and love. He cannot look forward to scenes of temptation and sorrow, through which covenanted mercy has engaged to bear him to the hour of death and the joys of a future world without a heart expanding with love for his heavenly Father. That God should show mercy to a wretch like him, angels have no such cause for gratitude as this!

A distinguishing characteristic of true love for God is that it is supreme. No man can serve two masters. There cannot be two objects of supreme regard. "He," said our Savior, "who loves father or mother more than Me is not worthy of Me." When God promised to circumcise the heart of His people, it was that they might love the Lord their God with all their heart and all their soul. God neither requires nor will accept of a divided affection. He is a jealous God. No rival may participate in that love which is due to Him. Genuine love to His character is something more than languid esteem, a mere lukewarm affection; it is something more than a vague, indescribable emotion that plays round the head. It is the ruling passion, the governing motive. The love of God is paramount to every other principle. Every attachment is subordinate to delight in His excellence; every desire is subservient to that of promoting His glory. To a mind that loves Him, God is equally the source and sum of good.

> Of all Thy gifts, Thou art Thyself the crown,
> Give what Thou wilt, without Thee we are poor,
> And with Thee rich, take what Thou wilt away.

But while we say that in every renewed heart the love of God is the predominant principle, we ought not to withhold the remark that it exists in very different degrees in different persons, and in the same persons, at different times. While the people of God remain in this probationary state, they will be sinners. Their love to God will be very unequal at different seasons, and at some, very low and languishing. The best of men have their seasons of sin, as well as their seasons of darkness. Sometimes they are on the mount, and sometimes in the vale. They are prone to forsake God; like Israel of old, they are bent to backsliding from Him. The glory of His character has little effect upon their hearts, and less upon their conduct. The honor of His name excites no ardent desire to promote it, no anxious concern to see it promoted. Other objects employ so much of their time, and engage so much of their affections, that for a while, they think more of things that are seen and temporal, than of those that are unseen and eternal.

By a state of probation, I do not intend to involve anything that bears the remotest resemblance to the unscriptural notion either that all mankind are not, by the apostasy of Adam, brought into a state of sin and condemnation, or that those who were chosen in Christ Jesus before the world began are in a state that renders their final perseverance in the least degree uncertain. A state of probation is a state of trial, in order to a righteous retribution. In the present world, men have a fair opportunity to form their characters for eternity. They are not in a state of probation in the same sense in which Adam was placed in that state. They are not under a covenant of works. The question to be tried is not whether they shall stand or fall by that covenant. But they are under a dispensation of grace. If, while in the present world, they repent and believe the gospel, they may look for the blessed hope and glorious appearing of our Lord Jesus Christ. But if, while in the present world, they remain impenitent and unbelieving, they will heap up wrath against the day of wrath and revelation of the righteous judgment of God. Unbelievers enjoy this dispensation of grace in common with believers. They have a reprieve from final condemnation, together with the opportunity of fleeing to Christ for a complete reversal of the condemning sentence. Believers also enjoy a dispensation of grace in common with unbelievers. They are kept only through faith unto salvation. God has placed them in a world where they must watch and pray; where they must forget the things that are behind and reach forth toward those which are before; where they must keep their body under control and bring it into subjection lest by any means they should be cast away. A state of probation, therefore, is neither inconsistent with the infallible certainty of the saint's final perseverance, nor the sinner's present condemnation.

But there are seasons also when the child of God, gradually excluding all other objects from his view, fixes his mind upon the divine character as the object of his chief delight, and upon the divine glory as the great end of his being. There are seasons, seasons of inexpressible sweetness and delight, when, like Elijah on Carmel, Moses on Pisgah, and John in Patmos, he is lost in the contemplation of the ever-blessed God, and borne aloft to catch a glimpse at that glory that fills the temple above. He beholds the Infinite One arrayed with majesty and excellence, and decked with light as with a garment. He beholds the bright and brightening displays of His glory, while his bosom expands with holy fervor and beats high with pure devotion.

It is not necessary to inquire whether the state of declension or of vigor is the more desirable, nor which it is our duty to avoid and which to cherish and maintain. Both the duty and blessedness of God's people point to that heavenly precept, "Be ye perfect, even as your Father in heaven is perfect." I do not ask the reader whether he possesses that degree of love which he ought to possess, but whether he possesses any that is genuine. "I love them," said the voice of eternal wisdom, "that love Me." The holy God cannot love those who hate Him. He cannot regard those with complacency who regard Him with aversion. He cannot be reconciled to those who are unreconciled to Him. He cannot be reconciled to those who hate Him, and who justify their hatred to Him. He retains His anger toward them so long as they retain their opposition and enmity toward Him.

I am happy in being able to quote the words of a divine so deservedly eminent as [Peter] Van Mastricht, in confirmation of a truth that meets with so much opposition from the popular theology of the present day. He said, "Our complacency in God will in return excite God's complacency in us." The inference is unavoidable: God's complacency in us does not precede, but follows our complacency in Him.

Hence none have a right to believe that God loves them until they first love Him. And none will believe it without having been given up to strong delusion that they should believe a lie. A man must be conscious of his love for God before he can have scriptural evidence of God's love for him. And the evidence that arises from this consciousness is conclusive. We have no more right to doubt God's love for us than we have a right to doubt our love for Him. As our love for God grows constant and vigorous, the evidence increases that we are friends to God, and that God is a friend to us.

The reader may perhaps ask how this is reconcilable with the declaration in 1 John 4:19, "We love Him because He first loved us"? God's love for His people is the cause of their love for Him, but it is not the motive of their love to Him. It precedes their love to Him in these two respects:

1. He loved them with the love of benevolence, as He did other men. He sent His Son to be the propitiation for their sins.

And but for this expression of benevolence, the whole human race would have been abandoned to the ruins of the fall. There would have been no gospel, no way of reconciliation, and consequently not a vestige of holy love in the barren world.

2. He loved them with the love of election. He gave them to His dear Son in the everlasting covenant. In pursuance of His gracious design, He makes them new creatures, slays their enmity, and sheds abroad His love in their hearts. And but for this expression of distinguishing love, they would have forever remained His enemies. "I have loved thee with an everlasting love," says God to His Church, "therefore with loving-kindness have I drawn thee."

In these respects, the love of God for us is the cause of our love for Him. It cannot be the motive of our love to Him for this plain reason, that we have no evidence of His distinguishing love for us until we possess the consciousness of our love for Him.

The love that God exercises toward the elect while they are yet in their sins is of a peculiar character. It cannot be the love of complacency, for it is exercised while the objects of it are perfectly hateful, and is therefore consistent with the utmost detestation of their whole characters. It cannot be the love of benevolence, for the love of benevolence is impartial, and this is discriminating. It is very properly called the "love of election."

I am happy to present the reader with a correct view of this text, from an author who may justly claim more than a common share of confidence. Hear Thomas Scott:

"They who serve God from filial affection, not slavish fear, love Him because He first loved them; not that their love is merely gratitude for His previous benefits, which, abstracted from other exercises of love, would be a very selfish affection; nor could any man in that case love God at all on good grounds, without some immediate revelation to assure him that he was the object of His special love, even while he had no grace and was wholly impenitent and sinful. But the evident meaning is that if the Lord had not loved them before they loved Him, even when they were dead in sin, they must forever have continued enemies to Him. His love suggested the plan, and provided the means of redemption. He revealed to sinners His glorious perfections and abundant mercy in the Person and work of His Son. He sent His Word to declare to sinners this great salvation, and to invite them to partake of it. He regenerated them by His Spirit, and so brought them, by repentance and faith in Christ, into a state of acceptance and reconciliation; and thus taught and enabled them to love His excellence, to value His favor, to be thankful for His inestimable benefits, and zealous for His glory. As, therefore, His love for them was the original source of their love for Him, so from the latter they may infer the former, and take the comfort of the happy change that has been wrought in them, while they give Him the glory of it."

Is then your heart right with God? Are you pleased with the divine character? Do you love every part of that character? Do you love God's holiness as well as His grace, His justice as well as His mercy? Do you love Him because He is immutably disposed to hate sin and punish the sinner, or merely because He is disposed to forgive sin and save the sinner? Do you love Him because He has a greater regard for His own glory than your happiness, or because you apprehend that He has a higher regard for your happiness than for His own glory? There is a kind of love that flows from a very unworthy principle. "If ye love them that love you, what thank have ye; for sinners also love those that love them." To love God from no higher motive than the persuasion that you are interested in His favor is supremely selfish. Those who love God from no higher principle do not love Him at all. This is the affection that might and does reign without opposition in the hearts of thousands who are far from righteousness, and who will finally be excluded from the kingdom of heaven.

Are you reconciled to that character of God that you see portrayed on every page of His Word? Are you well-pleased that God should not only possess that character; but are you well-pleased that all His perfections should be under His own direction and control? Do you love God as a sovereign God? How do you regard the manifestation of that character in the distinguishing dispensations of grace and justice? Do you approve it, or do you oppose it? Do you love it, or do you hate it? Everything that God does, everything that He eternally designed to do, is an expression of what He is. Everything that He does in fixing the eternal allotments of the righteous and the wicked is a display of His true character. To be opposed to what He does, therefore, or to be opposed to what He eternally designed to do, or to object to His designing from eternity to do anything is to oppose God, and to object to His divine excellence. Whenever any part of the divine character, clearly understood, is the object of opposition and hatred rather than of acquiescence and delight, the opposition is the result of selfishness and malignity—and those who cherish it do not have the love of God in them.

Is the glory of God the great end of your being? Do you sincerely and ardently desire to see greater and brighter displays of that glory? Do you rejoice that God is unfolding, and will forever unfold, the excellence of His character? Do you know nothing of this benevolent regard for God and the interests of His kingdom? Do you find your happiness in yourself, or out of yourself? Do you rejoice merely in the hope of your personal interest in God's favor, or do you rejoice in the hope of His glory? Can you unite your feelings with His, your joys with the joys of His people, and share in the blessedness that results from beholding the ever-blessed God completely and forever glorified?

What has your experience taught you of the love of gratitude to God? Do you behold God in all your mercies? Do you feel that you live in God's world, that you breathe God's vital air, that you are upheld by God's powerful hand? Do you delight to feel the sweet and tender obligations that bind you to the Lord Jesus Christ? Have you seen the seasons when the abundant goodness, the infinite grace of God towards you, a polluted sinner, seemed enough forever to fill your heart with love and your lips with praise?

Is your love for God supreme? Does it rise superior to the attachments of flesh and sense? What, whom, do you love more than the everlasting God? In whose character do you behold more beauty? Whose blessedness is an object of warmer desire or more vigorous exertion? To whom are you more grateful? Do you love God more than father or mother, wife or children, houses or lands? Do you love Him better than yourself? "If any man come to Me, and hate not his father, and mother, and wife, and children, and brethren, and sisters, yea, his own life also, he cannot be My disciple."

There may be danger, but surely there can be no necessity of being deceived in a case so plain. Supreme love for God is decisive evidence of the renewed heart. When the soul is ushered from the darkness of sin into God's marvelous light, it beholds God in an infinitely different light from what it ever beheld Him before. Now, God is everywhere. There is an inexpressible beauty, a mild glory in almost every object, because it is the work of His hand and reflects the excellence of His nature. The language of those who love God is that of the rejoicing Church: "I will greatly rejoice in the Lord; my soul shall be joyful in my God." They think how excellent a being God is, and how exalted would be the happiness to enjoy Him to perfection, and to be swallowed up in Him forever. To see and to love that which is infinitely lovely, to behold and to adore that which is supremely adorable, is the character and the blessedness of the heavenly world. The early dawn of this spiritual light, the first glow of this pure affection, is the glimmering of that sacred fire that will burn with a purer and a brighter flame throughout interminable ages.

Does the reader then love God? If so, the question as to his own good estate is at rest. If you are a friend to God, God will be an everlasting Friend to you. Nothing shall separate you from His love. Neither angels, nor principalities, nor powers, nor things present, nor things to come, nor height, nor depth, nor any other creature shall be able to separate you from the love of God that is in Christ Jesus your Lord.

7

Repentance

The fall of Adam involved both himself and his posterity in sin and ruin. From the moment of the first transgression, sin challenged universal empire. From that fatal hour it began to assume dominion, with the certain prospect of swaying its scepter over every climate and every heart. But blessed be God, though its empire is universal, it is not everlasting in all its extent. There is One who takes the prey from the mighty. The conqueror is vanquished. Though sin reigns unto death, grace reigns unto eternal life.

A mere glance at the ruin and recovery of man is enough to convince us that of the religion of fallen beings, repentance forms an essential part. It is equally significant of the character and indispensable to the happiness of a converted sinner to be penitent.

In the order of gracious exercises, repentance follows love for God. An affectionate view of God prepares the mind to take a just view of sin. As it is impossible to repent of having sinned against a God whom we hate, so it is impossible not to repent of having sinned against a God whom we love. When the heart has been renewed, when the soul, enlightened by the divine Spirit, sees the beauty, the loveliness of the divine character, it cannot seriously reflect upon a life of sin without unfeigned grief. "Godly sorrow worketh repentance to salvation, not to be repented of; but the sorrow of the world worketh death."

Genuine repentance is that sorrow for sin that arises from a sense of its intrinsic turpitude.

It is essential to the nature of godly sorrow that we possess a settled conviction of the evil of sin. It is not enough to have merely a transient view of our sinfulness; we must possess a settled conviction of the great evil of sin. The real penitent, though he has reason to lament that he is never so deeply affected with the view of his sin as he should be, seldom so much so as he hoped to be, and very frequently not affected at all, yet at some favored seasons he is enabled to view it in a measure as it is. He sees its detestable nature. He is deeply impressed with a sense of its turpitude as a violation of law. This is the definition that the apostle has given of sin: It is the transgression of law. The God who made all worlds, and who alone is qualified to govern the worlds that He has made, has given a rule of action to His creatures that is the result of infinite wisdom and goodness. The precept and the sanction of this law are perfectly equitable. The highest authority has pronounced them to be holy, just, and good.

To violate this law is an evil. To violate this law is nothing less than an attempt to sunder the bond that holds the moral world together. It is therefore a great evil. Every violation of this law is an effort to resist the salutary effects of a perfect rule of action. It is a virtual opposition to all the good that that rule of action, if obeyed, would eventually secure. Could the evil nature and tendency of sin therefore be fully expressed, could this enemy of all righteousness be clothed with the energy of omnipotence, all that is good, all that is happy, would be chased away, and the world that once smiled under the beneficent hand of its Maker would be left bare of the last vestige of bliss. This is the same accursed foe that hurled the angels from the highest heavens, that drove our first parents from paradise, that deluged the world by a flood, that laid waste the cities of the plain, that has multiplied its trophies in slaughtered thousands, that has given death its sting and the law its curse, that has crucified the Lord of glory, would not stay his ruthless hand until he had rolled the volume of desolation through the empire of the Eternal, and enjoyed the malignant pleasure of brooding over the ruins of the desolated universe.

In violating the law, sin also dishonors the Lawgiver. It aims the blow at God. It rises in rebellion against His rightful authority. It is contrary to every attribute of His nature. It is the abominable thing that His soul hates. To enhance its turpitude, think a moment against what a God sin is committed. He is a great God, a God of infinite majesty. He is decked with majesty and excellence. The everlasting mountains are scattered at His approach; the perpetual hills bow before Him. He is a holy God, so holy that the heavens are not pure in His sight, and His angels are charged with folly. He is a good God. He is love itself. He is a merciful God. His mercy is everlasting; it is great unto the heavens. He is the Being whom we are under the greatest obligations to adore because He is supremely adorable; a Being whom we are under the greatest obligations to love because He is infinitely lovely; a Being whom we are under the greatest obligations to obey because His government is perfect. And yet we rebel. Creatures whose foundation is in the dust contend with their Maker! Creatures who hang every hour upon His bounty forget His power and abuse his love! Sinners who are upheld every moment by His mercy tread that mercy under their feet! Oh, how great an evil is sin! If one man sins against another, the Judge shall judge him; but if a man sins against God, who shall entreat for him!

Thoughts in kind like these pass through the mind of the penitent, as he calls to remembrance his multiplied transgressions. No longer does he make light of sin. He views it in an entirely different light from that in which it is viewed by a thoughtless world. To him it is odious; it is vile; it is utterly detestable; nay, more, it is exceedingly sinful.

In view of the intrinsic turpitude of sin, therefore, the penitent mourns. And his sorrow is ingenuous. It is not a selfish sorrow. The object upon which the soul fixes her thoughts, while indulging her grief, is sin and not punishment. It is for this that she mourns. This, in the hands of the divine Spirit, is the spring of all godly sorrow.

The leading principle that makes repentance a duty is that evil has been done; a crime has been committed. To the renovated heart, this is also the leading motive to repentance. No truth is more clear than that sinners ought to be, and that saints are, penitent for sin. The inherent odiousness of sin is the object of their sorrow; and were this the only consideration that could be presented to the mind, this alone would be enough to clothe them with eternal mourning and bathe them in ceaseless tears. We cannot refrain from saying that neither the obligation nor the motive to repentance are founded in the hope of mercy, or the actual exercise of it, though both are thereby strengthened. Notwithstanding, both the obligation and the motives to repentance are vastly increased by the proclamation of mercy in the gospel; yet men must repent, and do repent, because they have done wrong, and not because there is or is not a probability that they shall escape punishment. The moment that our first father fell, before he heard the voice of God among the trees of the garden, while under the fearful apprehension, nay, the certain expectancy of the rigid execution of the curse, he was under the immutable obligation to repent. The fallen spirits in hell are now without excuse for not humbling themselves before God. Though bearing the punishment of their iniquity, yet in view of the intrinsic turpitude of their sin they ought to be overwhelmed with unfeigned sorrow.

The reader will perceive that these remarks are made with the design of distinguishing between that sorrow of the world that works death and that godly sorrow that works repentance to salvation not to be repented of. In the world that lies in wickedness, there is enough of that sorrow that works death. There is the sorrow that arises merely from a sense of danger and the fear of punishment. Such was the repentance of Ahithopel and Judas. But this is at an infinite remove from that godly sorrow that works repentance not to be repented of. It is one thing to mourn for sin because it exposes us to hell, and another to mourn for it because it is an infinite evil. It is one thing to mourn for it because it is injurious to ourselves, another to mourn for it because it is offensive to God. It is one thing to be terrified, another to be humbled. A man may tremble at the apprehension of divine wrath while he has no sense of the intrinsic turpitude of sin, and no true contrition of soul on account of it.

There is also the sorrow that arises merely from the hope of forgiveness. Such is the mercenary repentance of the hypocrite and the self-deceived. Many, it is to be feared, have eagerly cherished the expectation of eternal life, and here begun and ended their religion. Many, it is to be feared, have eagerly cherished the hope of mercy, and here begun their repentance, who have mourned at the last and lain down in sorrow. In all this there is nothing that is ingenuous, no godly sorrow arising from a sense of the intrinsic turpitude of sin.

Real repentance is also deep and thorough. It is bitter sorrow. It rends the heart. The penitent sees that he is a vile sinner. He sees that he has been his own destroyer. The Spirit of God has taught him that sin is something more than a mere calamity. He feels that he deserves to be blamed rather than pitied. He views his sin as altogether criminal and inexcusable. Though the dictates of an evil heart have often prompted him to go astray, yet he knows they have never constrained him contrary to his own choice. That heart, though full of evil and desperately wicked, he has cherished. He sees therefore that he himself is the only blamable cause of his sinfulness. The great evil of sin is chargeable upon him. He has done it.

And can the penitent see his own vileness without bowing in the dust before God? He is ashamed and confounded when he looks back upon his past life, and when he now looks into his own heart. He sees that he has broken God's holy law and resisted the claim of his rightful Sovereign. The thought that most deeply affects him is that he has sinned against God. In comparison with this, his other crimes vanish to nothing. The language of his heart is, "Against Thee, Thee only, have I sinned!" If he had not sinned against a great, a holy, a good, and a merciful God, his sins would not appear so great. But, oh, he has sinned against the God who made him, the God who has preserved and redeemed him. Creating goodness, providential care, and redeeming love have been bestowed upon him almost in vain. This is the dart that wounds him. He exclaims with David, "I have sinned against the Lord! I have committed this great wickedness!" He sensibly feels that he has sinned against the God of all grace. He beholds Him whom he has pierced; he looks away to the cross of Christ, and there sees what his sins have done, and is grieved to the inmost soul.

The number of his sins affects him no less severely than the aggravation of them. The penitent sees that he has not only sinned, but sinned in a thousand forms. He sees sin in a thousand things in which he never saw it before. It appears to mix itself with almost everything. He groans under the body of sin and death. At some periods he goes bowed down to the earth all the day long. He feels that his transgressions are multiplied. Often his laughter is turned into mourning and his joy into heaviness. With what a melting, broken heart does he lie at the feet of his injured Savior and beg for mercy. He is abased before God. He is ready to cry with the humbled Psalmist, "My sin is ever before me!" or with the mourning prophet, "O my God, I am ashamed, and blush to lift up my face to Thee; for mine iniquities are increased over my head, and my trespass is grown up unto the heavens!" It is enough to break his heart seriously to reflect upon his innumerable transgressions. He remembers his own ways and his doings that were not good, and loathes himself in his own sight for his iniquities and abominations.

True repentance is not only ingenuous and deep, it is attended with actual reformation. It exhibits itself in real life. The penitent feels the force of considerations that never fail to restrain from sin. He is afraid of sin. He dreads its aggravated guilt. "How shall I commit this great wickedness, and sin against God!" The thought is enough forever to cut him off from all access to the accursed thing. He is a sinner still; but he cannot remain a sinner in the sense in which he was a sinner once. He manifests a desire to honor the God he has so long dishonored, to undo what he has done against the interest of His kingdom, and repair the injury he has caused to the souls of men. There is no genuine repentance where there is no forsaking of sin. Still to go on in sin, to practice iniquity with greediness, with constancy, and with perseverance, is incompatible with the nature of that sorrow that is unto salvation.

With these plain principles in view, I think the reader may decide the point as to his own good estate. The preceding observations will go far toward enabling him to distinguish between the precious and the vile.

If yours is godly sorrow, it is then ingenuous. It arises from a sense of the intrinsic turpitude of sin. Retire into your own bosom, therefore, and ask yourself questions like these:

Do I possess any settled conviction of the evil of sin? Does sin appear to me as the evil and bitter thing? Does a conviction of the evil of it increase? There are moments when heaven and hell lie out of sight. How does sin appear then? Do you hate it because it is merely ruinous to your soul, or because it is offensive to God? Do you hate it because it is sin? Do you mourn over it because it is wrong?

In the sanctified heart the hatred of sin is supreme. As there is nothing so bad as sin, so there is nothing the penitent hates so much. Is then your repentance deep and sincere? Is sin prevailingly your greatest grief? Seriously considered, would the deliverance from any evil be a more joyful event than the deliverance from sin? If there could be no deliverance from sin but at the expense of the choicest comforts, would you cheerfully make the sacrifice? Do your misfortunes grieve you more than your sins, or your sins more than your misfortunes?

Do your sins appear many and aggravated? Do you see sin in a thousand different forms, and new instances, in which you have not dreamed of it before? Do you mourn over the sins of the heart? Do you abhor yourself for your innate depravity, as one who was shaped in iniquity, and conceived in sin? Do you mourn over your vain thoughts and carnal affections; over a life of sin, ingratitude, and profligacy; over your unprofitableness and unfaithfulness? Does it grieve you that you are worldly, proud, and selfish; that you have lifted up your soul unto vanity, and panted after the dust of the earth?

Does it grieve you to the heart to call to mind that you have sinned against God? When your eyes behold the King, the Lord of Hosts, are you constrained to exclaim, "Woe is me!" When you look on Him whom you have pierced, are you constrained to cry out, "I am undone!"

The degree of godly sorrow is by no means to be overlooked in your self-examination. When God touches, He breaks the heart. Where He pours out the spirit of grace, they are not a few transient sighs that agitate the breast; they are heart-rending pangs of sorrow. "And it shall come to pass," said God, "that I will pour upon the house of David, and upon the inhabitants of Jerusalem, the spirit of grace and of supplication; and they shall look upon Me whom they have pierced, and they shall mourn for Him as one mourneth for an only son, and shall be in bitterness for Him, as one that is in bitterness for his firstborn. In that day, there shall be a great mourning in Jerusalem, as the mourning of Hadadrimmon, in the valley of Megiddon. And the land shall mourn, every family apart; the family of the house of David apart, and their wives apart; the family of the house of Nathan apart, and their wives apart; the family of the house of Levi apart, and their wives apart; the family of Shimei apart, and their wives apart; every family apart, and their wives apart. Thus have the Jews mourned, and thus will that devoted nation mourn again, for crucifying the Lord of glory."

Does the reader know anything of such sorrow as this? Can no solitary hour, no lonely spot, bear testimony to the bitterness of his grief? What grieves you more than that you have ten thousand times pierced the heart of redeeming love?

Do you abhor sin? Do you turn from it? Do you cherish that regard for the law and character of God, that tender regard for the crucified Savior, that inspires you with fixed aversion to all that is polluting in the sins of the heart, and all that is injurious in the sins of the life? Do you feel an increasing tenderness of conscience whenever you are tempted to go astray? Are you afraid of dishonoring God, and do you tremble lest you crucify His dear Son afresh?

Fellow sinner! If you know anything of all this, you are not a stranger to that godly sorrow which works repentance to salvation not to be repented of. God has promised to forgive the penitent. He has pledged His word that the act of forgiveness on His part shall follow the exercise of repentance on yours. Returning prodigal! Pardoning mercy is yours. It is as sure as the sincerity of your repentance. "Whoso covereth his sins shall not prosper, but whoso confesseth and forsaketh them shall find mercy." His repentance shall not purchase it; his repentance does not deserve it. Repentance has no intrinsic efficacy. It cannot entitle to pardon. It is not the Savior, though without it we cannot be saved. God delights to forgive. He does forgive, though it cost the blood of His Son. No sooner does the rebel loathe and abhor himself than God passes by his transgressions and ceases to retain His anger. He rejoices over him with joy. He rests in His love. He will joy over him with singing. To forgive a hell-deserving sinner, to receive a rebel into favor, to wash away his deep-stained guilt, and become the everlasting friend of the friendless, is the highest exercise of perfect benevolence. Oh, how gratifying to the benevolent heart of God to behold the returning prodigal, though a great way off! His compassions yearn over him. He longs to receive him into His arms. He is impatient to press him to His bosom. He runs. He falls upon his neck and kisses him.

8
Faith

The first glimmering of light that dawned upon the darkness of the fall was ushered in by an obscure revelation of the covenant of grace. This covenant was faintly exhibited to Adam and Eve in the denunciation of the curse upon the Tempter. It was made known more clearly to Noah after the flood. It was renewed with Abraham after God had called him from Ur of the Chaldees; with Isaac in Gerar, with Jacob, at Bethel, and with the generation of Israel in the wilderness. The light of truth rose gradually, and the covenant of grace gradually unfolded its blessings till the Star of Bethlehem pointed to the Sun of Righteousness, and the promise of the covenant was sealed by the blood of its Surety.

There is an important distinction between the covenant of redemption and the covenant of grace. The period of their formation, the parties, the terms of these several covenants, are perfectly distinct.

It is unhappy that there should be a difference in the mode of representing this subject among divines that are reputed to be orthodox. The view that is given of it by an eminent divine of the Presbyterian Church may not be unimportant in this place and day:

> There seems to be mention made in Scripture of a covenant or agreement between the Father and the Son. This the generality of Calvinistic divines consider as a separate or preparatory contract, and call it "the covenant of

> redemption." Some, however, especially those who have
> been termed "antinomians," consider this as properly the
> covenant of grace, made with Christ the second Adam, as
> representing His spiritual seed; and the covenant said to be
> made with believers to be only the execution or
> administration of that covenant, and therefore called a
> testament, being the fruits of Christ's death, or ratified by
> the death of the testator. (John Witherspoon's *Introductory
> Lectures on Divinity*)

This distinction cannot be considered as an invention of the
New School. It will be found expressly recognized by [Peter] Van
Mastricht, and I think, clearly implied by [Frances] Turretin.

The covenant of redemption was formed from eternity, the
covenant of grace in time. The covenant of redemption was
antecedently necessary to the existence of the covenant of grace.
It was the perfect accomplishment of that arduous part that the
Redeemer engaged to bear in the covenant of redemption that
laid the foundation for the covenant of grace. It was this that
justified God in entering into covenant with believers, and in
engaging to save them through faith in the blood of Jesus.

The covenant of redemption subsists between the sacred
persons in the ever-blessed Trinity, of which the atonement of
Christ for the sins of the world is the stipulation, and the
salvation of His chosen seed the promise. The covenant of grace
subsists between God and believers, of which faith in Christ is
the stipulation, and the salvation of believers the promise.

The covenant of grace, therefore, in distinction from the
covenant of redemption, is nothing more or less than the
promise of God to save all those who believe in Jesus Christ.
The law of God is not now the rule of justification, though it is
the rule of duty. We no longer hear the righteous demand of
that broken covenant, "This *do*, and thou shalt live," but the

milder language of gracious economy, "Believe, and thou shalt be saved." Of this covenant, faith in Christ is that part which is fulfilled by the believer. He believes and, upon the principles of this covenant, the first act of faith gives him a humble claim to the promise.

Every Christian grace is the effect of the immediate agency and the Almighty power of God upon the heart. Faith is expressly declared by the apostle to be the gift of God, though it is at the same time the act of the creature.

Every Christian grace is the gift of God and, at the same time, the act of the creature. The dependence and the activity of man are perfectly reconcilable. God works in man, but He works in him both to will and to do. In the day of God's power, His people are made willing. The enmity of the heart is slain, and they are made willing to do what they were unable to do before.

If any one will take the trouble to turn to Scott's *Family Bible*, he will find the following sentiment in his remarks on Romans 8:7-8: "Because the carnal mind is enmity ..." etc.

"This carnal mind is not subject to the divine law, and indeed cannot be so; it is morally unable to do any thing but rebel against it, and refuse obedience to it."

The observations of the same author on John 6:44, "No man can come," etc. are of the same import:

"The ground of this impossibility lies in the contrariety which subsists between the proud, worldly, unholy, rebellious, and ungodly nature of fallen man, and the humbling, spiritual, holy nature of the gospel. The gospel finds none willing to be saved."

Let the reader also advert to President Witherspoon's *Essay on Justification*. In volume 1 of his *Works*, he will find the following paragraph:

Since mention has been made of perfect conformity to the will of God, or perfect obedience to His law, as the duty of man, which is indeed the foundation of this whole doctrine [that is, the doctrine of justification], I think it necessary to observe that some deny this to be properly required of man as his duty in the present fallen state because He is not able to perform it. But such do not seem to attend either to the meaning of perfect obedience or the nature or cause of this inability. Perfect obedience is obedience by any creature to the utmost extent of his natural powers. Even in a state of innocence, the holy dispositions of Adam would not have been equal in strength and activity to those of creatures of an higher rank; but surely to love God, who is infinitely amiable, with all the heart, and above all to consecrate all his powers and faculties without exception and without intermission to God's service, must be undeniably the duty of every intelligent creature. And what sort of inability are we under to pay this? Our natural faculties are surely as fit for the service of God as for any baser purpose. The inability is only moral, and lies wholly in the aversion of our hearts from such employment. Does this then take away the guilt? Must God relax His law because we are not willing to obey it?

The same great man, in a sermon on the absolute necessity of salvation by Christ, has also a sentence that is full of meaning: "For I hope no Christian will assert that any person in the world who has the exercise of reason is not under a natural, but only a moral impossibility of coming to the knowledge, and doing the will of God. If the first were the case, it would take away all sin; but the last is such an obstinate disinclination as is still consistent with guilt and blame." Witherspoon's *Works*, volume 2, p. 357, Philadelphia edition.

The following representation of the subject I take the liberty of giving to the public, principally because it is from an unexpected quarter. It is extracted from a "Catechism adopted by the Consistories of the Reformed Dutch Churches in the town of Rhinebeck, for the use of their people, and published by their order."

Q. Why do men thus break and transgress the law of God?

A. The reason is the reigning aversion of their hearts to it, so that they are unable to keep it.

Q. And does not this their inability release from obligation?

A. No, for it is of such a nature as tends not in the least to break or weaken our obligation.

Q. Of what kind is it then?

A. It is not of a natural, but of a moral kind.

Q. What is natural inability?

A. Natural inability consists in a defect of rational faculties, bodily powers, or rational advantages.

Q. What is moral inability?

A. Moral inability consists in a want of a proper disposition of heart to use our natural ability aright.

Q. Can you illustrate the distinction by producing an instance?

A. Yes, the case of Joseph's brethren who hated him so, that they could not speak peaceably to him.

Not viewing this sufficient, the Catechists then subjoin the following note:

> Thus we say of a man destitute of an honest principle, that he cannot refrain from cheating you if he has an opportunity; that some are such profane wretches that they cannot open their mouths without an oath; and others are such liars that they cannot speak the truth; that some are so revengeful that they cannot forgive an injury; and others so easily provoked that they cannot keep their temper if you contradict them. So a carnal mind cannot be subject to

God's law; for a man who hates God cannot serve Him, cannot rejoice in seeing Him glorified, cannot love His image, cannot see any comeliness in Christ, nor fall in with the gospel plan of salvation. The difference between moral inability and that which is termed "natural" is plain and self-evident. It is said of the mariners that they rowed hard to bring the ship to land, but they could not (Jonah 1:13); also of Joseph's brethren, that they could not speak peaceably to him. In the former case there was a natural, in the latter a moral inability. Thus the inability of Zacharias to speak (Luke 2:22) was widely different from that mentioned in 1 Samuel 25:17.

The importance of a proper attention to this distinction appears when we observe that the former releases from obligation, but the latter does not. It was no crime in Isaac, being old, that he could not see (Genesis 27:1); but the case seems very different with those who have eyes and see not (Jeremiah 5:21), or such as have eyes full of adultery, though it is expressly said of them that they cannot cease from sinning (1 Peter 2:14).

On this subject, the reader may also consult Watts' *Ruin and Recovery*, and also his *Liberty and Necessity*.

He may also turn to Charnock's *Works*, volume 2, p. 137; and Edwards on *The Freedom of the Will*, Part 1, Section 3d.

Faith is uniformly represented as of the operation of God. It is one of the fruits of the Spirit. The fruit of the Spirit is love, joy, long-suffering, gentleness, goodness, *faith*. No man can say that Jesus is the Lord *but by the Holy Ghost*. It is expressly said of those who believed on Christ in the days of His humanity that they were born, not of blood, nor of the will of the flesh, nor of the will of man, but of God. It is also unequivocally declared that whosoever believes that Jesus is the Christ is born of God. Faith, then, is the exercise of the new heart.

It is difficult to give a definition of faith that comprehends all its properties. In its most general character, it is reliance upon the testimony of God's Word. It is receiving the truth in the love of it. The Apostle Paul uses the phrase "received not the love of the truth" as synonymous with the phrase "believed not the truth." Faith, however, when viewed as that evangelical grace which is the condition of the New Covenant, possesses altogether a peculiar character. Though the elementary principles of every evangelical grace are involved in that love which is the fulfilling of the law, yet every grace has a specific form. Faith, strictly speaking, is distinct from every other exercise of the renewed heart. It is not love, nor repentance, nor humility, nor submission, nor self-denial, nor hope. It is indeed the exercise of a heart that already loves God, and that is humbled on account of sin; but it is one that takes that view of the gospel of Jesus Christ, which is taken by no other grace.

One of the best definitions of faith will be found in the Shorter Catechism of the Assembly of Divines at Westminster. In answering the question, "What is faith in Jesus Christ?" they say, "Faith in Jesus Christ is a saving grace whereby we receive and rest upon Him alone for salvation as He is offered to us in the gospel."

Faith in Jesus Christ is a complex act of the mind, and comprises several distinct things. One of its properties is a true knowledge of Christ's character. It is impossible to "receive and rest upon" a Being whose character we do not know, and whose character we do not know to be worthy of confidence. "I know whom I have believed," said the Apostle Paul. Faith views the Lord Jesus as He is. It discerns the divine excellence and majesty of His character. It recognizes the child who was born in Bethlehem as the Mighty God, the Everlasting Father. The proper divinity of the Savior's character is one of those plain principles of the gospel that are essential to evangelical faith. To make an all-sufficient atonement for sin, to soften the obdurate heart, to aid the believer in his trials and sufferings, to defend him from the power and subtlety of his enemies, and to bring him off a conqueror at last would baffle the designs of all but Eternal Wisdom, and mock the power of all but an almighty arm. Faith views the Savior as truly divine. None other than the eternal Word made flesh can be the foundation of hope, for none other can be mighty to save. It is presumption to profess to know Christ without acknowledging Him as the second of the three co-equal persons in the Godhead.

As the believer discerns the Lord Jesus as He is, he also acknowledges Him as a real and proper man. He views Him as He is represented by the apostle, to be the one God and one Mediator between God and men, the *man* Christ Jesus. It is expressly said that Christ did not take on Him the nature of angels, but the seed of Abraham. The acknowledgment of Christ as man as well as God cannot be separated from the true knowledge of Him as He is revealed in the Bible. There He is represented, and there He must be viewed, as encircled with all the majesty of the self-existent God, and all the milder glories of the man Christ Jesus.

The believer regards Christ in His whole mediatorial character. He sees the fullness, the perfection of His work, no less than the divine excellence of His person. He has respect to all the offices of Christ. He views Him as the prophet who came to publish the will of God and declare the way of salvation. He views Him as the priest, whom it became God to institute, and sinners to possess; as the One whom God has set forth to be a propitiation, through faith in His blood, to declare His righteousness for the remission of sins that are past, that God "might be just, and the Justifier of him that believeth in Jesus." He views Him as the King in Zion, the Head over all things to

His Church, the Lord Jesus, the lord who bought him. In Christ, the believer discovers all that can qualify Him to be a Savior, and all that can encourage guilty, miserable man to trust in His grace. In Him, he beholds One who is eminently all-sufficient, One who is able, willing, and faithful to save to the uttermost. He receives the record that God has given of His Son.

Sincere love to the character of Christ is also essential to the nature of genuine faith. It is as impossible to receive and rest upon a being whom we hate as it is to receive and rest upon one that we do not know. Faith in Christ is not an exercise of the understanding merely; it is an affection of the heart. With the heart man believes. "If thou believest *with all thy heart*," said Philip to the Eunuch, "thou mayest be baptized." To those who believe, Christ is precious. The excellence that they see both in His person and in His work, they love. All that they know of Christ, they love. All the truth that is connected with the character and work of Christ, they love. They possess spiritual discernment of His divine excellence. They have the single eye that discovers His moral beauty. They see a loveliness in Christ and His gospel that captivates their hearts. When the wandering spouse was met by the watchmen who went about the city, and was accosted with the unexpected inquiry, "What is thy beloved more than another beloved?" the reply was: "My beloved is the chief among ten thousands, He is altogether lovely."

Abraham rejoiced to see Christ's day; and he saw it, and was glad. The pious Psalmist was enraptured with a view of His loveliness. "Thou art fairer," said he, "than the children of men; grace is poured into thy lips, therefore God hath blessed Thee forever."

The spirit of this language is not peculiar to David or Abraham. In the dignity, purity, and amiableness of Christ's

character, in the design of His mission, and in the way of
salvation by His cross, every believer sees enough to engage his
sweetest and most exalted affections.

With this acquaintance with the character, and this
attachment to the person of the Redeemer, the believer
"receives and rests upon Him alone for salvation, as He is
offered in the gospel." He makes an implicit surrender of his
immortal soul into His hands, as to One who is both able and
faithful to save. The yielding of the soul to the disposal of Christ
is an act of the mind that cannot be separated from living faith.

It is of some importance to bear in mind that faith is the act
of a lost sinner seeking deliverance from the power and
punishment of sin, toward a Being who is exhibited in the
character of a Deliverer. It cannot, therefore, imply less than an
application of the soul to Him who is the delivering character;
the actual adventuring of this vast concern with Him, together
with the hope that with Him it will be secure. Faith receives
Christ; it rests upon Christ for salvation; it rests upon Him
alone for salvation, as He is offered in the gospel. Sensible of his
ill-desert and helplessness, persuaded of the all-sufficiency of the
Redeemer, the believer therefore makes a voluntary surrender of
himself into the hands of Christ to be saved upon His own
terms. He is convinced of the necessity of committing his cause
to better hands than his own. He relinquishes his vain
confidences, and places all his hopes on Christ. He casts himself
into His arms. "Lord, to whom shall I go but to Thee!"

In the act of surrendering the soul into the hands of Christ,
the believer takes a view of the Great Deliverer, which is as deep
as his own wants, and as large as the provision that is made to
supply them. He receives Christ as his Prophet, his Priest, and
his King.

Is he ignorant, exposed to wander from the path? The Great

Prophet is his Teacher and his Guide. The meek He will guide in judgment; the meek will He teach His way.

Is he polluted with sin? He looks to the blood of the spotless sacrifice to be cleansed from all sin. Jesus Christ he knows gave Himself for His Church that He might wash and cleanse it. He rests on Him, and looks for the sanctification of the spirit unto obedience only through the sprinkling of the blood of Jesus.

Is he guilty and condemned? No longer does he trust his own righteousness, but looks to Jesus as the end of the law for righteousness to everyone who believes. He yields a condemned soul to Him to be arrayed with a righteousness with which a just God has declared Himself to be ever well-pleased. He rests upon Him as the sole ground of acceptance. With all his natural attachment to his own goodness, he counts it loss for Christ. He counts it but dung that he may win Christ, and be found in Him, not having his own righteousness which is of the law, but that which is through the faith of Christ, the righteousness which is of God by faith. This is his refuge, his crown of rejoicing. He looks to Jesus, recognizing the high relationship in which He stands to His people, and the endearing name by which He is called, "JEHOVAH OUR RIGHTEOUSNESS."

Is he weak and helpless? He engages the grace of the Redeemer as his consolation and strength. To Jesus he surrenders himself as the Head of all divine influences. "I live, yet not I, but Christ liveth in me." This is the language of faith. The act of the soul in surrendering itself into the hands of Christ forms a connecting bond between Him as the Vine and the soul as the branches, which communicates life, strength, nourishment, and beauty. In a word, with a just view of the character, and a supreme attachment to the person of Christ, the believer yields himself into His hands as a full and complete Savior. Him he receives; upon Him he rests, and rests for time and eternity. With humble joy will he tell you, "Christ is my all. I want no more. To Him I look to be sanctified by His Spirit, to be governed by His laws, to be protected by His power, to be saved by His death, to be disposed of at His pleasure, and to be the means of promoting His glory."

This is what it is "to receive and rest upon Christ alone for salvation, as He is offered to us in the gospel." This is confidence in Jesus Christ as a divine Savior. You cannot possess these feelings without possessing saving faith. This is the substance of things hoped for, and the evidence of things not seen. This is the grace that renders invisible things visible, future things present, and stamps the permanent idea of reality upon everything that rests upon the testimony of God. This was the faith of Old Testament saints and New Testament saints. It is that trust in the Lord of which we read so often in the Old Testament, which is nothing more nor less than the confidence of the new born soul in God, as reconcilable through the Mediator.

Thus have we seen that faith has properties peculiar to itself. Its character is perfectly distinct from every other grace. There is no exercise of the renewed heart that views the whole gospel plan as it is except this. Faith, from its essential nature, implies the fallen state of man, while it recognizes the principles of the covenant of grace. It is itself the condition of that covenant[*]. It

---

[*] When the author calls faith a condition of the New Covenant, he does not mean that it is the meritorious ground of acceptance with God. The covenant of grace bears no resemblance to a contract, in which the part to be performed by the believer is a mere *quantum meruit*. Every principle of that covenant rests upon the fact that man is unworthy, and that salvation is all of grace. When we say, therefore, that faith is the condition of the New Covenant, we mean that faith is that act of the creature, wrought in him by the agency of the Holy Ghost, without which, according to the tenor of the New Covenant, there is no salvation—it is a *sine qua non*.

is a grace that is alike distinguishable from the love of angels and the faith of devils. It is peculiar to the returning sinner. None but a lost sinner needs, and none but a humbled sinner relishes, the grand sentiment of faith, that grace reigns through righteousness unto eternal life, by Jesus Christ our Lord.

Here then let the reader examine himself whether he is in the faith. He may possess the faith of devils. He may be fully persuaded that there was such a person as Jesus Christ, that he was delivered for our offenses and rose again for our justification. He may possess the vain confidence of the hypocrite, which neither works by love nor is of the operation of God; he may cherish the pernicious hope of the self-deceived while he remains blind to the excellence of the divine character, and while enmity to the cross of Christ is the governing principle of his heart and his life. Every carnal mind, whether sensible of it or not, maintains the most decided aversion to the person of the Redeemer, the benefits of His purchase, and the terms upon which those benefits are proffered. The whole character and work of Christ bear so intimate a relation to the unbeliever, they so pointedly take the part of God against him; they so unequivocally condemn his character and conduct, they will have such a damning efficacy upon him throughout eternal ages, that when clearly seen they cannot fail to draw forth the latent enmity of his heart.

If it is true, as it unquestionably is, that you may have a just view of the character of Christ while you have no love for that character as infinitely deserving your affection, and while you make no surrender of yourself into His hands, as to one who is supremely worthy of your confidence, it becomes you to inquire whether you love the Lord Jesus in sincerity and truth, and whether you trust in Him as your only foundation of hope.

"Simon, son of Jonas, lovest thou Me?" Apply the question.

Do you love Christ? And why do you love Him? Do you love Him merely because He died to save you, or because He died to honor God in your salvation? Do you love Him because He descended from heaven to take the part of God against man; to show the world that in the contest between the creatures and the God that made them, God is right and man is wrong, and with His own blood to set His seal to the truth that the soul that sins ought to die? Or does He appear to you on this account, as a root out of a dry ground, as having no form nor comeliness, no beauty that you should desire Him? The true believer loves the Lord Jesus because He effects his eternal salvation in a way that harmonizes with the glory of the divine character. To be saved in a way that is in the least reproachful to that glory would rob Heaven of its sweetness. It is for this that Jesus Christ is so precious to those who believe; in this, that He is eminently fairer than the sons of men. Do you love Jesus for the divine glories of His person, for the excellence of His life, for the benefits of His death, for the prevalence of His intercession, for His resurrection, His dominion over the world, and His office as the Supreme and Final Judge? Are the feelings of your heart drawn out toward Christ as your chief joy? Can you sit down under His shadow with great delight, and find His fruit sweet to your taste? When affected with a view of your lost state and guilty character, when bowed down under a sense of sin, does Christ appear precious? Is a view of Him refreshing?

Do you receive the Lord Jesus, and rest upon Him alone for salvation? Can you take the place of a lost and hell-deserving sinner, and with a broken, contrite heart, make an implicit surrender of your immortal soul into His hands to be saved upon His own terms? Beloved reader, this is a plain question. Every humbled heart, in the exercise of faith, knows how to answer it. Can you relinquish every other hope? Can you adventure this vast concern with Him?

Can you receive and rest upon the Lord Jesus as He is offered in the gospel? Are you at heart reconciled to the terms of the gospel? Are you at heart reconciled to the humbling doctrine of being justified by faith in the righteousness of Christ? It is a doctrine that, if correctly understood, will be seen to reduce the returning rebel to the lowest point of degradation. To a heart that is invincibly attached to rebellion, it is hard to bow. To one who is naturally attached to his own supposed goodness, it is hard to renounce it all, and desire and receive mercy only for the sake of Christ. To a man who loves himself supremely, and values himself supremely, who has cherished the most extravagant notions of his own importance from the womb, it is hard to lie down at the footstool of sovereign mercy. It is cutting indeed to the pride of the human heart to be constrained to feel that we are guilty, and then forced to admit that there is no pardon for our crimes but through the merit of another.

Say, reader, is your heart bowed to the humbling terms of the gospel? Do you delight to take your place at the foot of the cross, and while reaching forth the hand to receive the robe of the Savior's righteousness, to shout, "Grace! Grace! Not unto me, O Lord, not unto me, but unto Thy name be the glory, for Thy mercy and truth's sake?" If so, you believe. If so, amidst all your doubts and fears, you have that faith which is the gift of God. If so, you may humbly claim the promise. Here is your consolation: He who believes shall be saved. Yes, shall be saved! What more has God to bestow; what more can the creature enjoy? Here are blessings as great as the capacity of the immortal soul, as eternal as the God who engages to bestow them. In the comprehensive promise of that covenant to which faith makes you a party, the mysteries of eternity lie concealed. Life and death, earth and heaven, things present and to come, joys high, immeasurable, and immortal—what shall I say? All are yours; and you are Christ's, and Christ's is God's.

9

Humility

"In the school of Christ," said the devout Archbishop [Robert] Leighton, "the first lesson of all is humility; yea, it is written above the door as the rule of entry or admission. 'Learn of Me, for I am meek and lowly of heart.' " Humility is a grace that is nearly allied to repentance. Repentance respects the nature and aggravation of sin; humility respects the person and character of the sinner. Humility consists in a just view of our own character, and in the disposition to abase ourselves as low as the vileness of our character requires.

A just view of our own character is a view of it as it actually is. The pride of the human heart naturally casts a veil over the character of man, and aims to conceal his worthlessness as a creature and his deformity as a sinner. The humility of the gospel naturally throws aside the veil and reveals that native worthlessness which ought to sink the creature in the dust, and that moral deformity which ought to cover the sinner with confusion. Genuine humility is inseparably connected with a sense of our dependence, of our unworthiness, and of our ill desert.

Although dependence, absolute and universal, is necessarily attached to the very being of creatures, yet a sense of this dependence is a most unwelcome visitant to the unhumbled heart. The spirit of the carnal mind is an independent spirit. It is a spirit in which the pride of man glories. Though men are creatures of yesterday and know nothing, though they are upheld by the visitation of God's arm and supplied by the beneficence of His hand, they have no apprehension that they actually live, move, and have their being in Him. An abiding sense of His universal presence is what they cannot bear to cherish.

But a sense of perfect dependence is a grateful guest to the broken and contrite heart. To a humbled sinner it is sweet to feel that he is absolutely dependent on God for all that he is and all that he has. He is sensible that he is nothing, that he is a worm and not a man. He realizes that God is everywhere, and that worms and seraphs are equally at His disposal. He feels with Paul that he is not sufficient of himself to think any thing as coming from himself, but that his sufficiency is of God. Does he enjoy signal favors? He calls to mind that he enjoys nothing that he has not received. Life, health, as well as the blessings of both, he sees flowing through a thousand channels from the same exuberant source. As the child hangs upon the kindness of its parent, or as the abject poor depend on the daily bounty of their fellow men, so do the poor in spirit, conscious of their helplessness, wait only upon God, for their expectation is from Him.

With a sense of their dependence, the humble unite a conviction of their unworthiness. They are unworthy, and they feel that they are so. They are sensible that they are sinners. They have seen the plague of their own hearts. They know, at best, that they are unprofitable servants, and at best ought to be forever overwhelmed with a sense of their unworthiness. Merit, they have none. Deserving of good is not in all their thoughts. "Who am I?" exclaimed the King of Israel, "Who am I, O Lord God, and what is my father's house, that Thou hast brought me hitherto?" "I am not worthy," said the humble patriarch, "I am not worthy of the least of all Thy mercies, and of all the truth which Thou hast showed unto Thy servant!"

The people of God need not be told that they have forfeited every favor. Much as they need the divine compassion, they are sensible that they do not and cannot deserve it. Often as they seek the divine face and favor, they do not seek them as the reward of personal worthiness. They turn their thoughts inward, and see and feel that they are less than the least of all saints. They are mere pensioners upon sovereign mercy. There was no distinguishing excellence in them that made them the objects of favor; there was not the shadow of difference in character which operated as a reason why God should regard them with the special tokens of His love rather than the most abandoned wretch who ever lived? "Behold, 1 am vile! Grace has made me to differ." When they seek the presence of God, they do it with the humble spirit of the centurion: "Lord, I am *not worthy* that Thou shouldest come under my roof!" When they cast themselves upon the care of their heavenly Father, it is with the spirit of the prodigal: "Father, I have sinned against heaven, and in Thy sight, and am *no more worthy* to be called Thy son!"

In the humble heart, a sense of dependence and unworthiness is also connected with a sense of ill-desert. Humility holds up to view the bright mirror of God's holy law. From this faithful glass the character of man is reflected in all its native deformity. Here there is no deception. The merit and demerit of character are determinately fixed by this impartial standard. Here God has exhibited His right and our obligation, His righteousness and our ill-desert. Weighed in this unerring balance, the character of man is found wanting. It is the character of a transgressor. It is the character of a rebel against the King of heaven, a character that is condemned, cursed, and is in its own detestable nature deserving of everlasting wrath.

Unfeigned humility prompts a man to view his character as

base, and himself as ill-deserving, as the law of God views them. The humbled heart knows that the law is holy, and the commandment holy, just, and good. He not only feels that the wages of sin is death, but approves the law that threatens him with death for every transgression. He not only sees that sin and guilt are inseparably connected, but approves of the Lawgiver for hating and punishing sin according to its desert. He prostrates himself in the dust, and exalts God on the throne. He takes his proper place at the footstool of God's amiable and awful sovereignty. He knows that he ought to lie as low as vindictive justice can reduce him. He feels that it is of the Lord's mercies that he is not consumed. Such is his sense of ill-desert that he not only feels that he is justly condemned, but magnifies the justice that condemns him while he adores the grace that rescues him from the condemnation.

Such is the view that the humble man takes of his own character. This is to think soberly of himself, and as he ought to think. This is to have just views of his own character, and voluntarily to abase himself as low as the vileness of his character requires him to lie. This is the disposition with which he renounces his own righteousness and relies on the righteousness of the Lord Jesus Christ. Once the humble man thought little of his own vileness; now a sense of his vileness covers him with shame. Once he thought himself to be rich and increased with goods, and in need of nothing; now he sees and feels that he is wretched, miserable, poor, blind, and naked. Once he was too proud to become a beggar; now he begs for mercy, begs with hope and with joy in the name of Jesus.

This is the disposition that is interwoven with his experience and his conduct. It manifests itself both toward God and toward man. Especially it manifests itself toward God. When thinking of God, when beholding His glorious perfections, when rejoicing in the perfection of His government, and in the excellence of His designs, the humble heart adopts the language of Job: "I have heard of Thee by the hearing of the ear, but now mine eye seeth Thee; wherefore, I abhor myself, and repent in dust and ashes." When thinking of God, he feels the weight of obligation to love and serve Him with all the heart. Hence he is borne down under a sense of his inexcusable deficiencies. A view of his corruption keeps him near to the earth. He is ashamed that he is no more holy. How often is he constrained to exclaim, "O wretched man that I am! Can it be that one who knows no more of the love of God, who is no more conformed to His image, is in truth His own dear child!" He desires to divest himself of all his pride, to empty himself, to feel as nothing, and be as nothing and vanity.

In the more immediate presence of God, the humble Christian remembers that he is a redeemed sinner. When approaching the mercy seat, he takes the place of a broken-hearted beggar. He goes to the God of all grace like a man who knows that he deserves to sink into hell. He is ready to bow low before Christ, to wash His feet with his tears, and to wipe them with the hair of his head. Like the woman of Canaan, he begs for the crumbs of divine mercy. He does not desire to plead his own merit, but with a bosom bleeding for sin, and an eye cast down to the earth, makes mention of the name of Jesus. Though at times he is ashamed to approach the throne, though he hardly dares approach, yet like the publican, standing afar off, he does not so much as lift up his eyes to heaven, but smites upon his breast, saying, "God, be merciful to me, a sinner." His most favored moments are those in which he is enabled to lie low before a holy God, and in which he has increasing desires to be kept humble to the end of his days.

This humble temper of mind also naturally flows forth in

his intercourse with his fellow men. It is true that some good men have vastly more native haughtiness, vastly more of the overbearing spirit of the carnal man to struggle with than others. Notwithstanding this, real Christians are humble; and their humility will necessarily express itself in the modesty and meekness of their habitual deportment. "Let nothing," said the Apostle Paul, "be done through strife or vainglory, but in lowliness of mind let each esteem other better than themselves." The spirit of Christianity is congenial with its precepts, though it is not in the present life perfectly conformed to them. There is such a thing as "in honor preferring one another," though we may sometimes be led to imagine that there is not much of it visible. There is such a spirit; and however those who indulge the hope of their good estate may be disposed to shrink from the test, such is the spirit of all Christians.

"Charity," said the apostle, "vaunteth not of itself, is not puffed up, doth not behave itself unseemly." With a humble frame of mind, a man will set a due value upon his own attainments. He will not be apt to think highly of his own virtues, nor consider himself injured if he is not highly esteemed by others. It is difficult for an unhumbled, self-righteous man not to betray his hypocrisy by being proud of his supposed self-abasement. He has much to say of his frames and experiences, much to boast of the abasing views that he has had of himself, and the wonderful discoveries in divine things with which he has been favored. But the truly humbled soul desires more to be humble than to appear humble. It is no part of his character to make great pretenses to humility. There are indeed seasons when he is favored with unusual manifestations of the divine glory, and abasing views of his own vileness. And he sometimes speaks of them. With modesty he may speak of them. He is not freed from the duty, nor deprived of the privilege of telling what the Lord has done for his soul, merely because the world may brand him with the name of "Pharisee." But when he does it, it is that he may strengthen the weak, refresh the weary, cheer the desponding, and give honor to divine grace. He does it not boastingly, not with the language, "God, I thank Thee that I am not as other men," but with the spirit that esteems others better than himself. He knows that he has nothing to be proud of, and that if he is made to differ from others, it becomes him to adopt the language of the Psalmist rather than that of the Pharisee, "Not unto me, O Lord, not unto me, but unto Thy name give glory, for Thy mercy and Thy truth's sake!"

Something like this is the spirit of the gospel. A sense of dependence, of unworthiness, and of ill-desert, manifesting itself both toward God and toward man, is the spirit of humility. When the Christian, as the elect of God, puts on bowels of mercies, kindness, humbleness of mind, meekness, long-suffering, then he exhibits the power and sweetness of vital religion. Seated in the lowest place, and clothed with humility, he exhibits some degree of the amiableness of his divine Master. Well may we call humility a heaven-born grace. She is indeed the daughter of the skies, the "meek-eyed child of Jesus," and dwells only with him who, like herself, is born from above.

Here then you have a rule of trial. The spirit of humility is conclusive evidence of vital godliness. It enters into the essence of religion. Here the new nature eminently discovers itself. The humble spirit is that child-like, Christ-like temper which is exclusively the effect of the almighty power of God upon the heart.

Can the reader lay his hand upon his heart and say that he is conscious of this heavenly temper of mind? Can he, in the sincerity of his soul, say that he is conscious of this spirit of voluntary self-abasement? Did he ever, and does he still, take a just view of his own character, and does he possess the disposition voluntarily to abase himself as low as the vileness of his character requires him to lie?

Do you cherish a conviction of your dependence? Or do you live without God in the world? Do you live from day to day, and from year to year, realizing the relation that you bear to the great First Cause? Do you delight to feel that God sees you, upholds you, and governs you? Or do you banish a sense of your perfect dependence upon Him, and feel and act as though God had no concern with you, and you had no concern with Him?

Do you cherish a sense of your great unworthiness and ill-desert? Do you feel yourself to be a vile and hateful sinner? What if others should esteem you according to the vileness of your character; would you not view yourself injured? If God should esteem you, and treat you according to the vileness of your character, would you not think it hard and unjust? Would you not murmur and complain?

Is the humble temper of the gospel interwoven with your religious experience? A savor of humility is diffused throughout all the Christian graces. "Christian affections," said the immortal [Jonathan] Edwards in his *Religious Affections*, "are like Mary's precious ointment, that she poured on Christ's head, that filled the whole house with a sweet odor. It was poured out of a broken box; till the box was broken, the ointment could not flow. So gracious affections flow out of a broken heart. Gracious affections are also like those of Mary Magdalene, who also pours precious ointment on Christ out of a broken alabaster box, anointing therewith the feet of Jesus, when she had washed them with her tears and wiped them with the hair of her head. All gracious affections that are a sweet odor to Christ, and that fill the soul of a Christian with a heavenly sweetness and fragrance, are brokenhearted affections. A truly Christian love, either to God or men, is a humble, brokenhearted love. The desires of the saints, however earnest, are humble desires. Their hope is a humble hope, and their joy, even when it is unspeakable and full of glory, is a humble, brokenhearted joy, and leaves the Christian more poor in spirit, and more like a little child, and more disposed to an universal lowliness of behavior."

Is the humble spirit of the gospel also interwoven with your habitual deportment? Are you habitually disposed to esteem others better than yourself, or to esteem yourself better than others? Do you rejoice to see others of equal merit with yourself as much beloved and honored as you are? And if their merit exceeds your own, are you willing to see them more beloved and honored than you are? Or are you forever restless and dissatisfied because you are not more beloved and honored than everybody else? Do you love the praise of men more than the praise of God? "How can ye believe," said the meek and lowly Jesus, "how *can* ye believe, who receive honor one of another, and seek not the honor that cometh from God only?"

In the character of a Christian, humility is the one thing needful. Where this is wanting, all is wanting. A proud, haughty spirit is inconsistent with the spirit of the gospel. It is the genius of that gospel, it is one grand design of all the dispensations of grace toward fallen man, to exalt him to glory by first humbling him in the dust. "He that exalteth himself shall be abased, and he that humbleth himself shall be exalted."

Does the reader indulge the hope of having made his peace with God? Let him remember that God is at peace with none except the humble and contrite. "He lifteth up the meek, but casteth the wicked down to the ground." No matter what are your professions, no matter how high your supposed attainments, if you have never felt the contrition of a broken heart, you have never tasted that the Lord is gracious. Still, you are not to reject the hope of your good estate because you find much of the spirit of pride within you. Alas, how much of this detestable spirit have the best of God's people! With this enemy will be our longest and severest conflict. It possesses so much of the cunning of the Serpent that it is perhaps less easily detected than any other form of depravity. When you have mortified it in one shape, you will find that it rises in another; and when you fondly hope it is dead, you will find that it has been secretly gathering strength to commence the attack with new vigor, fresh courage, and perhaps greater success. Pride will live until the old man is dead. It is the ulcerated part of the body of sin and death. It is the main spring to all the obstructions that impede our progress toward heaven. It is the secret avenue through which the Tempter too often enters and leads the best of men astray. It is the great inlet of the smoke from the bottomless pit, which darkens the mind, casts a gloom around their fairest prospects, and sometimes leaves them a while in the gloom of despondency.

With this enemy will be your longest and severest conflict. Put on, therefore, the whole armor of God, and watch unto prayer. The clashings of pride and humility should often drive the Christian to the throne of grace. "Who can understand his errors? Cleanse Thou me from secret faults!" You may have much pride; but have you any humility? Be not deceived. "Seest thou a man wise in his own conceit? There is more hope of a fool than of him. Blessed are the poor in spirit, for theirs is the kingdom of heaven."

10
Self-Denial

From the formation of the first angel of light down to the period when the heavens shall pass away as a scroll, the Creator of the ends of the earth had His eye steadfastly fixed on the same grand object. As all things are of Him, so all will be to Him. He who made all things for Himself cannot fail to pursue the end for which He made them, and to obtain it at last. When the proceedings of the Last Day shall have been closed, when the assembled worlds shall have entered upon the unvarying retributions of eternity, when the heavens and the earth shall have passed away, and a new heaven and a new earth, the Holy City, the New Jerusalem, shall have come down from God out of heaven, He who sits upon the throne shall say, "It is done. I am Alpha and Omega, the beginning and the end!"

In winding up the scene, it will appear that God Himself is the first and the last; not merely the efficient, but the final Cause of all things. The vast plan, which has for its object nothing less than the brightest manifestation of the divine glory, has an inalienable right to the most unreserved devotedness of every intelligent being. To the advancement of this plan, God therefore requires every intelligent being to be voluntarily subservient. All the strength and ardor of affection that we are capable of exercising must be concentrated here. Every faculty, every thought, every volition, every design, must be devoted to this great cause. The injunction is explicit: "Whether therefore ye eat, or drink, or whatsoever ye do, do all to the glory of God."

Now the heart of depraved man is obstinately averse to such a course of feelings and conduct. Instead of being supremely attached to God, and the good of His kingdom, men are by nature lovers of their own selves. Hence there is a controversy between man and his Maker. God requires men to regard His glory as the great object of their affections, and the ultimate end of their conduct; but they disregard His requisitions, and in all their feelings and conduct have respect ultimately to themselves. This controversy draws the line of distinction between friends and foes. As the spirit of self-advancement is the root of all sin, so the spirit of self-denial is the root of all holiness.

Self-denial consists in the voluntary renunciation of everything that is inconsistent with the glory of God and the highest good of our fellow men. It does not imply the voluntary renunciation of good, or the voluntary toleration of evil, as being desirable in themselves considered, though it does imply both as being desirable all things considered. There is no absurdity in the proposition that a thing may be very unpleasant in its own nature, but, taking all things into view, may be very desirable. It is perfectly consistent for men to desire to enjoy themselves, and yet desire to deny themselves; to hate misery, and yet be willing to suffer it. Neither does it imply the renunciation of all regard to one's self. The desire of happiness and the aversion to misery are inseparable from human nature. The natural principle of self-love does not constitute the sin of selfishness. A man may have a due regard to his own happiness without being supremely selfish. There is no moral turpitude in being influenced by the anticipation of good or the apprehension of evil, provided I am not influenced by these considerations supremely. There is no sin in regarding my own interest, provided I do not put a higher estimate upon it than it will bear. The evil lies in viewing it of greater importance than it is, in making every thing subservient to myself, and myself subservient to nothing.

Self-denial is diametrically opposite to supreme selfishness. "Selfishness," says Dr. [John] Owen, "is the making a man's self his own center, the beginning and end of all that he does." It is difficult, with the Bible in our hands, or upon the principles of sound philosophy, not to acknowledge the distinction between affections that are supremely selfish, and truly disinterested, to be both plain and important. There is no need of the aid of metaphysical discussion to establish the proposition, that no man ought to regard his own happiness more than everything else, and that the man who does possesses none of the spirit of the gospel. The affections of men must be placed on some one object that is paramount to every other. Two objects of supreme delight there cannot be. Two paramount principles of action there cannot be. There is no intermediate object between God and self that can draw forth the highest and strongest affections of the soul. As there is no such thing as a creature's going out of himself without rising as high as the glory of God, so there is no such thing as a creature's going out of God without descending as low as himself. Other objects may be loved; but if they are not loved merely as the means of self-gratification they are not loved supremely. Affections that do not terminate on God terminate on self. Men who do not seek the things that are Jesus Christ's seek their own. Inordinate self-love is the ruling passion of their hearts, and the governing principle of their lives. They love themselves not as they ought to love themselves, but supremely. They set up their own private good as the highest object of desire and pursuit. Their affections operate in a very narrow circle. They have no ultimate regard but to themselves. They have but one interest, and that is their own. A supreme regard for their own happiness is the main spring of all that they do for

God, of all that they do for themselves, and all that they do for their fellow men.

It is needless to say that with this spirit Christian self-denial has no communion. The nature of this heavenly grace is expansive. It is the result of a supreme attachment to a higher interest than our own. It lights on self, but does not terminate on self. It stops at nothing short of the highest good and, in pursuing that, terminates on an object large enough to gratify the strongest desires of the most benevolent mind. He who is not a stranger to the spirit of self-denial has learned to make his own interest bend to the interest of God's kingdom, and that from supreme regard to the interest of God's kingdom, and not from supreme regard to himself. The glory of God is the great end of his conduct. It is his great concern that God should be glorified, that His laws should be obeyed, His gospel loved, and the highest interest of His infinitely extended kingdom prevail and triumph. Once he denied Christ for himself; now he denies himself for Christ. Once he lived for himself; now he lives for God. No duty is so hard that he is not willing and resolved to perform, no sin so sweet that he is not willing and resolved to forsake. He takes up the cross at the hazard of everything. Nothing is too dear to give to Christ; nothing is too great to be cheerfully sacrificed for the promotion of His glory. Such is the disposition of good men that they place their happiness in the glory of God and the prosperity of His kingdom. They delight in this, in itself considered. They love and pursue this for what it is in itself considered, and not merely for the happiness that will result to them from pursuing it. And the spirit of disinterestedness will irresistibly impel them to do so*. The glory of God the

---

*If the opposition of the present day to the use of the word "disinterestedness" did not strike deeper than at the name, we would be

chargeable with great incivility in not abandoning the use of it. But we cannot abandon the truth—no, never! Once let the Christ-like spirit of disinterestedness be reduced to the level of mere selfishness, and the maxims of Godwin, Bolingbroke, and Hume will harmonize with the maxims of Edwards, Paul, and Jesus Christ. It well became an infidel to say, "Self-love is the only spring from which all moral duties and affections flow." It well became the apostle to say, "Charity seeketh not her own." Here their systems differ. Here their characters differ. This is the point of difference between the precious and the vile. Systems and characters that diverge here, and that continue to diverge, will find the impassable gulf between them at last.

It is unhappy that plain Christians should have imbibed the notion that the doctrine of disinterestedness is an innovation. It is not true. It is a doctrine of the Reformation, a doctrine well understood and clearly taught by the divines of the fifteenth and sixteenth centuries. The leading principles of that doctrine as exhibited in this essay do not differ from the views of [John] Calvin, [Peter] Van Mastricht, and [Herman] Witsius.

The great Witsius said, "The true believer does not strive to obtain holiness for the sake of human applause. He does not, by a mercenary self-love, aim merely at his own advantage either in this life or the life to come. The object of good men is far more pure and elevated, whereby they are carried out both toward God, themselves, and their neighbor. Above all things they seek the glory of God. This is the grand object of their affections. This they ardently desire and indefatigably pursue. "Let such as love Thy salvation say continually, 'The Lord be magnified!' " Hither, in all their exercises they tend, proceeding in an easy course until the day of Christ, being filled with the fruits of righteousness which are by Jesus Christ unto the glory and praise of God. As the source and principle of their works is the love of God, so the end of them is His glory. For he who loves God fervently loves above all things what is most beloved by God. But God so loves His own glory that whatever He does, He does with a view to promote it; so that all things are of Him that they may be again to Him, and to Him be the glory forever. In this respect the saints are like God, because in all their actions they have a supreme regard for His glory.

"In subordination to the glory of the divine name, the child of God may also, in the exercise of the Christian graces, have respect to himself, and endeavor to gain the assurance of his own eternal election—to rejoice in the testimony of a good conscience, and in that peace of mind that flows from

Christian must seek. Seeking this, he cannot be miserable; not seeking this, he cannot be happy. He knows he is but a point in the universe of God, an atom in the sum of being, a single member of Christ's mystical body; and he is willing that God should lift him up or cast him down at His pleasure. His own advancement is as a feather, a nothing, when put in the balance against the honor of Christ and the good of His kingdom.

Such is the spirit of self-denial. It is the result of a calm, deliberate, invincible attachment to the highest good, flowing forth in the voluntary renunciation of everything that is inconsistent with the glory of God and the good of our fellow men.

That this is the scriptural idea of self-denial it would be easy to illustrate by a multitude of examples. This is the elevated spirit that prompted the father of the faithful to offer up the son of promise, that bore the three worthies of Babylon to the burning fiery furnace, and that led the apostles and martyrs to glory in tribulation. It has borne the test of ridicule and reproach, stood undaunted before the scourge and the prison, triumphed amidst the light of the martyrs' fire, and smiled at the point of the sword. This is the spirit that shone with such signal luster in the sufferings and death of our Blessed Lord. It was eminently the characteristic of this divine Personage that in all He did and suffered He did not please Himself. He did not seek His own glory, but the glory of the Father who sent Him. "Though He was rich, yet for our sakes He became poor, that we through His poverty might become rich."

---

there. But evangelical holiness teaches so to desire these things as not to rest in them as our ultimate end, but to direct even them to the glory of God."

Vid. Hermanni Witsii, *de aeconomica foederum.* Lib. III. cap. xii. p. 478-81.

He often anticipated the day of His death, and, in itself considered, earnestly desired to be delivered from that fatal hour. He knew the malice of His enemies, and expected to feel the weight of it in His last sufferings. He foresaw all the circumstances that would add poignancy to His anguish, and foresaw them with distress and agony. But does He shrink from the dreadful undertaking? You see Him steadfastly setting His face to go to Jerusalem; you hear Him telling His disciples that He must go, He must suffer, and He must be killed—but do you hear Him complain? Go to Gethsemane, and there behold the Son of God under the most clear and awful view of His approaching crucifixion, and learn what it is to deny yourself for the sake of advancing the Father's glory. Listen to the language of a heart already broken with grief: "I am poured out like water; all my bones are out of joint. My heart is like wax; it is melted in the midst of My bowels. This body sweats, as it were, great drops of blood. The hidings of My Father's face are enough to bury me in eternal darkness. The guilt of this falling world will sink My feeble frame to the grave. O My Father, if it be possible, let this cup pass from Me! But now is My soul troubled. The hour is come, and what shall I say? Father, save Me from this hour! But for this cause came I to this hour. Father, *Glorify Thy Name!*" This was carrying self-denial to its highest pitch. So pure was the disinterestedness of the Savior that the sweetest feelings of His heart would have remained forever ungratified without the privilege of expiring on the cross.

This too is the spirit that is no less strongly enforced by precept than example. How often are believers exhorted *not* to seek their own, *not* to live unto themselves, and whether they live, to *live* unto the Lord; or whether they die, to *die* unto the Lord? That charity which the apostle represents as the distinguishing characteristic of believers is self-denying; it "seeketh not" her own. "If any man," said the divine Savior, "will come after Me, let him deny himself, and take up the cross and follow Me. Whosoever will save his life shall lose it, and whosoever shall lose his life for My sake shall find it."

One would think it difficult, after such an explication, to be long in doubt as to the nature of one of the most decisive evidences of real religion. We can hardly turn to a page in the Bible without being convinced that the grand distinction between true religion and false is that the one is disinterested, the other is supremely selfish. "For whether we are beside ourselves," said the apostle to the Corinthians, "it is *to God*; or whether we are sober, it is *for your cause*. For the love of Christ constraineth us, because we thus judge, that if one died for all, then were all dead; and that He died for all, that they which live should *not* henceforth live *unto themselves*, but unto Him which died for them and rose again." Those who are in the flesh, unbelievers, live unto themselves; those who are in the spirit, believers, live unto Christ. There are but two moral characters that are essentially different, and this is the radical difference between them.

Here then you have another criterion of Christian character. It is not supposed that in the present state we shall find self-denial unalloyed with selfishness. "There is not a just man upon earth that doeth good and sinneth not." Still, in the affections and conduct of every child of God, the spirit of self-denial is the prominent feature. He who possesses most of this spirit possesses most of the spirit of his divine Master. In the same proportion in which the glory of God and the welfare of His kingdom take the place of personal advancement, vital religion predominates in the soul.

I wish I could press this point upon the conscience of the

reader as closely as its importance demands. The end of the Christian in the exercise of grace is the glory of God, and not merely his own present or future happiness. The object at which he aims rises far above anything that is confined within the limited circle of which his little self is the center. Let the reader call in his wandering thoughts and inquire, "Have I ever been taught to fix my heart on anything infinitely more important than myself? Do not all my religious affections spring from some selfish motive? Is the desire of self-advancement, or the desire to advance the glory of God, the paramount principle of my feelings and conduct?"

The monastery and the cloister are not the only evidences that there is much of the show of self-denial where there is none of its spirit. We must look diligently into the nature of our religion if we would not be deceived. Men may deny themselves in a thousand instances from no other motive than that they expect to be the gainers by it. And no marvel, for Satan himself is transformed into an angel of light. You cannot know whether your self-denial is genuine, or whether it is spurious, without knowing whether it is founded upon a supreme attachment to the glory of God. To deny yourself from a supreme regard to a higher interest than your own is to possess the spirit of the gospel. Is this then the principle that regulates your conduct both toward God and toward man? Which do you pursue most, your interest or your duty? Which do you think of most, your interest or your duty? Can you sell all for the pearl of great price? Can you renounce your ease, your profit, your honor, when they come in competition with your duty? Can you renounce everything that is inconsistent with the glory of God, and the highest good of your fellow men? Are these the natural breathings of your heart: "Thy kingdom come! Thy will be done!" Is the highest interest of this kingdom identified with the object of your highest wish and your most vigorous exertion? Is the cause of Christ your concern, the dishonor of Christ, your affliction, the cross of Christ your glory? If so, you are not strangers to the spirit of self-denial. You are not without conclusive evidence that you are born from above. The more you forget yourselves in a supreme regard for God's glory, the more will you advance your own interest, both in this world and that which is to come. But the more you seek a selfish, private, separate interest, in opposition to the glory of God, the more are you seeking an interest that God has determined to destroy.

11

A Spirit of Prayer

Saul of Tarsus was once a hardened, obstinate sinner. He called himself "the chief of sinners," a blasphemer, a persecutor, and injurious. But he was a chosen vessel. It pleased God, who separated him from his mother's womb, suddenly to arrest him in his career, and, near the spot where he had anticipated the success of a commission armed with the most unrelenting virulence against the trembling Christians, to humble him to the dust. He had, in all its strength and prominence, borne the image of the earthly; but now he bears the image of the heavenly. "Behold," said the testimony of the faithful and true witness, "Behold, he prayeth!" He is not now the persecuting Saul, but the heaven-born, praying Paul. The proud Pharisee has become the humble suppliant; the stubborn rebel has become the meek child of Jesus. No sooner is the soul born than it breathes; no sooner is Paul converted than, behold, he prays!

When I say that the spirit of prayer is conclusive evidence of Christian character, I feel under obligation to point out wherein that spirit consists. We are not to forget that there is such a thing as drawing nigh unto God with the mouth, and honoring Him with the lips, while the heart is far from Him. The hearts of men may be as stupid and unfeeling, as proud and as self-righteous; they may be in the exercise of as sensible opposition to the character of the Most High, to the law and the gospel, while offering up the most solemn expressions of homage, as they are when God is not in all their thoughts. But it is not so with the righteous. His prayer does not go forth out of feigned lips. With the spiritual worshiper, the heart feels what the lips express.

The spirit of prayer is humble. It flows from a broken and contrite heart. The publican could not so much as lift up his eyes to heaven, but smote upon his breast, saying, "God be merciful to me, a sinner!" Before Him who is so great that the nations are as the drop of the bucket in His presence, and so holy that the heavens are impure in His sight, the suppliant feels as a man of unclean lips. Every sentiment of his heart constrains him to make the affecting confession, "O my God, I am ashamed, and blush to lift up my face to Thee; for my iniquities are increased over my head, and my trespass is grown up unto the heavens!" Sometimes a sense of guilt so overwhelms the soul as to prevent its free access to the throne. "Mine iniquities have taken hold upon me," said the Psalmist, "so that I am not able to look up; they are more than the hairs of mine head, therefore my heart faileth me."

The spirit of prayer is also believing. Numerous and aggravated as his sins appear, much as they attempt to discourage the believer from duty, he does not yield to the discouragement. He has respect unto the sacrifice of the Son of God. He believes that God is, and that He is a Rewarder of all who diligently seek Him. He looks to Jesus, the Mediator of the better covenant, as the way of access to the Father. The efficacy of His blood, the virtue of His righteousness is his only plea. He has an unshaken confidence that God can glorify Himself by answering his requests for Christ's sake, and he is therefore emboldened to press them in Christ's name. Though he has a lively sense of his own unworthiness, yet he knows that he has a Great High Priest who has passed into the Heavens, Jesus the Son of God, who is touched with a feeling of his infirmities; and he therefore comes boldly to the throne of grace that he may obtain mercy, and find grace to help in time of need. Until the work of redeeming grace shall cease; until the Father shall forget the Son of His love; until the name of Christ shall cease to be precious, and His intercession shall be no longer prevailing—faith in the blood of the spotless sacrifice will appertain to the nature of prayer.

But the spirit of prayer is also submissive. The suppliant prefers God's will to his own. This was the disposition that our blessed Lord manifested in the garden. It was an awful thought to Him to die; but it was a still more awful one that His Father's will should not be accomplished. Though Christ viewed the death of the cross in its own nature dreadful, yet he viewed the will of His Father delightful. He chose that His Father's will should be done rather than His own. "The cup which my Father hath given Me, shall I not drink it?" His will was absorbed in the will of God. "O My Father, *if it be possible,* let this cup pass from Me; nevertheless, not My will, but *Thine* be done!" This, in a greater or less degree, is the spirit of every genuine suppliant. He pours forth the fullness of his heart in the affectionate language of a child and the submissive language of a servant. He is prepared to be accepted or to be rejected in his petitions. He approaches the mercy seat with the desire that God would exercise His wisdom and grace in granting or denying his requests.

This is the spirit of prayer: sincere, humble, believing, submissive. Other prayer than this the Bible does not require, and God will not accept. This is the spirit of genuine devotion, a spirit that you cannot be conscious of possessing without the consciousness of your reconciliation to God. "Because ye are sons, God hath sent forth the spirit of His Son into your hearts, crying, 'Abba, Father.' " If you possess this spirit, though it is in a very imperfect state, you enjoy the high privilege of being adopted into God's family, and of occupying the place not of strangers, not of foreigners, not merely of servants, but of children, heirs of God and joint heirs with Jesus Christ. When the Spirit bears witness with our spirits that we are the children of God, how high the pleasure to utter our acknowledgments, to lisp our praise, to breathe forth our complaints toward heaven! What tongue can express the sweetness of these seasons of refreshing! How is the heart enlarged! Where the Spirit of the Lord is, there is liberty. No slavish fear perplexes the mind; no frown of divine displeasure guards the throne of mercy. The children of the common Father come near even to His seat. There they taste and see that the Lord is gracious; there they are assimilated into the likeness of the Holy One; there they see the clearest manifestations of the divine beauty, and beholding as in a glass the glory of the Lord they are changed into the same image, from glory to glory, even as by the Spirit of the Lord.

Does the reader possess the spirit of prayer? Is it his meat and his drink to hold communion with God through Christ, to have access by one Spirit unto the Father? Is it his greatest pleasure to be near to God, and his greatest grief to be far from Him? If so, however great his fears, he may have hope. His privilege is the privilege of sons; his consolations are those hidden joys with which a stranger does not meddle; his seasons of refreshing are foretastes of the river of life that flows from the throne of God and the Lamb.

It may not be amiss, while we are upon this subject, to spend a few minutes in looking at the question, "What evidence does the long continued practice of the external duty of prayer afford of the existence of vital religion in the heart?" I do not mean by this statement necessarily to exclude the spirit from the form of prayer. If we did, the question would be at an end. What evidence does the long continued practice of the external form afford of the existence of the internal spirit? It is a question of importance.

Men may pray much and yet not be Christians. They may pray in public and in their families and still not be Christians. This they may do to gratify their pride, to be seen of men, to maintain the character of Christians in the view of the world. They may pray in secret and not be Christians. But whether men persevere in the habitual practice of secret prayer without good evidence of Christian character is a question that I dare not answer in the negative. Neither would I venture to answer it unhesitatingly in the affirmative. This much the Bible will surely warrant us to say: Men who are not Christians will be exceedingly apt to neglect and, in the end, wholly to neglect the practice of secret prayer. Men do not act without motive. Now what motive can induce a man who is dead in trespasses and sins, whose carnal heart is enmity against God, to persevere in the habitual practice of secret prayer? Is it to silence the clamors of a guilty conscience? To do this he will pray, and often pray in secret. But will he always call upon God? The impenitent are sometimes the subjects of much seriousness; they are convinced of their duty and alarmed at their danger; and while they remain in this state they are compelled to admit the truth and importance of religion, and dare not omit the duty of secret prayer. But when they lose their convictions and forget their danger, the duties of the closet gradually become irksome. At length, they are weary. Conscience ceases to govern, and almost to accuse. Her monitory voice is silenced; and it becomes less and less difficult to cast off fear and restrain prayer before God.

There is another motive that will induce the impenitent to maintain the practice of secret devotion for a considerable length of time. Once they have wrought themselves into the persuasion that they are Christians, and have cherished the hope that they are interested in the blessings of the gospel salvation, they relinquish the persuasion, and abandon the hope with singular reluctance. They will do much to entertain and defend them. They are too selfish to omit a duty, the omission of which bears in its very face convincing evidence that they are hypocrites. They will rather practice the most self-denying duties, even long after they have lost their borrowed sweetness, for the sake of the testimony that they derive from this source that they are the children of God. This motive no doubt operates in many instances powerfully, and for some time; but does it operate uniformly, and to the end of life? With persons of this description, the omission of secret prayer is at first occasional, then more or less frequent as other avocations demand till at length the cares of the world, the temptations of the Adversary, and the allurements of sin so far blind the understanding and stupefy the conscience that the most hardened sinner still cherishes his vain confidence while he closes his eyes upon the last glimmering of evidence that that confidence is scriptural.

But though men may pray, and pray sometimes in secret, they will be exceedingly apt to neglect this duty if they are not Christians. Wherever you find the habitual performance of secret prayer for a long course of years, there is some reason to believe that you find the breathings of the newborn soul. There you may hope that there are hungerings and thirstings after righteousness. There you will usually discover a heart that is not in pursuit of hope merely, but grace; not safety only, but holiness. There you will usually, if not always, discover one not muttering over a few unmeaning sentences, as devoid of life as a loathsome carcass is of the life-giving spirit, but one whom the Spirit of God has taught to pray because he is weak and needs strength, because he is tempted and needs support, because he is in want and needs supply, because he is a sinner and needs mercy.

If these remarks are just, it is not impertinent to ask the reader whether he practices the duty of secret prayer? We do not ask whether he prays in secret now and then, whether he performs this duty on the Sabbath, or some occasional seasons of unusual alarm or solemnity? Is this his *habitual* practice? Has it been his habitual practice ever since he hoped he was brought out of darkness into God's marvelous light? No matter how punctual you are in other duties, no matter what evidence you have of your conversion from any other quarter, if you do not have this, you may set all the other things down as nothing. The want of this is decisive evidence against you, even if the possession of it is not decisive evidence in your favor. Prayer has been often styled "the Christian's breath." It is eminently so. A prayerless Christian! No, it cannot be. It is a mark of the highest delusion, of the grossest stupidity, to cherish the hope of having made your peace with God, and at the same time to live in the neglect of secret prayer. Who that has the least pretension to religion can presume to live without seeking the favor, without deprecating the wrath, and without realizing the presence of Him in whom he lives, moves, and has his being? To live without prayer is emphatically to live without God in the world.

Before I conclude this essay, I would give one caution to a certain class of readers. There is no want of those who live in constant doubt and trembling because they do not enjoy the constant presence of God, and the uniform fervency of affection in their retirements. Real Christians have seasons of coldness that chill the spirit of devotion. Such is the power of indwelling sin; so great is the influence of the world, the flesh, and the devil, that even God's own dear children are sometimes carried too far down the current. Yes, to the shame and guilt of God's people, we are constrained to make this affecting acknowledgment. Still, this humiliating truth does not militate against our general principle. Real Christians cannot live in the neglect of prayer; nay, more, those who do not possess the Spirit, and live in the habitual performance of the duty, are in the gall of bitterness and the bonds of iniquity. The moment a man begins to live in the neglect of prayer, that moment he should take the alarm.

May it then be said of you as it was of Saul of Tarsus, "Behold he prayeth!" If so, then you, like him, may be a chosen vessel. Maintain a constant and uniform intimacy with the throne of grace, and, for the sake of our great High Priest, God will put His fear into your hearts, and you shall not depart from Him. "Draw nigh unto God, and He will draw nigh unto you." Keep near to the fountainhead, and with joy shall you draw water out of the wells of salvation.

12
Love for the Brethren

The eminent Dr. [John] Owen, speaking of the primeval state of man, remarks that "the whole beauty of the creation below consisted in man's loving God above all, and all other things in Him and for Him, according as they participated in His glory and properties." That was a hopeless hour when the golden chain that bound God to man, and man to God and to each other, was broken. "Adam, where art thou?" Adam heard, and was afraid. The earth was cursed, and refused to yield her strength. Sin polluted all the joys of paradise; apostate man became the heir of misery, and henceforth dwelt in darkness, cherishing the seeds of malice and envy, hateful, and hating one another.

Upon this dismal gloom not a ray has dawned but from the cross of Christ. It is the prerogative of the gospel of Jesus to publish the glad tidings of great joy and, while it proclaims, "Glory to God in the highest," to restore peace on earth and good will to man. This gospel breathes the spirit of love. Love is the fulfilling of its precepts, the pledge of its joys, and the evidence of its power. "We know," said the apostle, "that we have passed from death unto life because we love the brethren."

The love of the brotherhood is not one of the native affections of the carnal mind. This cold, degenerate soil bears no such heavenly fruit. The affection that Christians exercise toward each other as Christians is the offspring of brighter worlds. It is a principle of celestial birth. Love is of God, and "every one that loveth is born of God, and knoweth God."

Brotherly love is an affection that is limited to particular characters. There can be no doubt but the children of God are kindly affectionate toward all men. Christian benevolence runs parallel with rational being. Genuine love for our neighbor is extended to all, according to their character and circumstances. It blesses those who curse us and does good to those who hate us. This, however, is not the distinguishing nature of brotherly love. Brotherly love differs materially from the love of benevolence. It is the love of good men, and for their goodness only. It extends only to the followers of Christ. It is an affection that is directed toward the excellence of religion. It is complacency in holiness.

There is something in the character of every child of God that reflects the image of his heavenly Father. It is this that attracts the eye and wins the heart. There is something that is amiable and lovely. And it is this loveliness that gives a spring to the affections and draws forth the hearts of God's people toward each other as they are drawn forth toward God Himself. The children of God are partakers of the divine nature. From bearing the image of the earthly, they now bear the image of the heavenly. God has imparted to them a portion of His own loveliness. He has formed them as new creatures. Of His free and distinguishing grace, He has made them, as they are called by the Wise Man, "more excellent than their neighbors." Hence they are lovely. They are the excellent of the earth. God loves them; Christ loves them; the Holy Spirit loves them; angels love them; and they love each other. It is around them that the virtues cluster; it is from them that the graces of heaven are reflected, though shaded, and very often darkened, by the most debasing and reproachful sins.

Love for the brethren is also an affection that rests upon the union that believers sustain with Christ. The Lord Jesus, together with all true believers, forms one mystical body. Christ is the Head and they are the members. "From Him the whole body, fitly joined together and compacted by that which every joint supplieth, according to the effectual working in the measure of every part, maketh increase of the body unto the edifying of itself in love." This union is represented by the apostle not only as the foundation of that communion which believers maintain with Christ, but of that which exists between believers themselves. The same bond that unites believers to Christ binds them to each other. The love that is exercised toward the Head extends to the members. The union itself necessarily involves a union of affection. Those who love Christ love those who are like Him, and those who are beloved by Him. Here all distinctions vanish. Name and nation, rank and party, are lost in the common character of believers, the common name of Christian. Jew and Gentile, bond and free, rich and poor, are one in Christ Jesus. They have "one Lord, one faith, one baptism, one God and Father of all, who is above all, and through all, and in them all." Actuated by the same principles, cherishing the same hopes, animated by the same prospects, laboring under the same discouragements, having the same enemies to encounter and the same temptations to resist, the same hell to shun and the same heaven to enjoy, it is not strange that they should love one another sincerely and often with a pure heart fervently. There is an unity of design, a common interest in the objects of their pursuit, that lays the foundation for mutual friendship, and which cannot fail to excite the harmony of souls. The glory of God is the grand object that commands their highest affections, and that necessarily makes the interest of the whole the interest of each part, and the interest of each part the interest of the whole.

They rejoice in each other's blessedness. There are no conflicting interests, and there need be no jarring passions. In a common cause, in a common cause that in point of importance takes the place of every other, and all others, the affections of the sanctified heart are one.

Love for the brethren, though in practice not always distinguished, yet in theory is easily distinguishable from all those affections and attachments that are purely natural. Men may love Christians merely because they imagine that Christians love them. This, like every other affection that is purely selfish, is unworthy of the Christian name. They may love particular Christians because they are of their party, and imbibe their sentiments. This too is nothing better than that friendship of the world that is enmity with God. They may esteem Christians merely from the force of education and habit. The people of God may not be the objects of contempt or aversion, and still they may not be the objects of complacency. Indeed our consciences may constrain us to respect them, the habits of early education may lead us often to associate with them, while we have no affectionate regard for the excellence of their character.

That love which is excited toward Christians as Christians is a constituted proof of saving grace. The reader will do well, therefore, to examine his own heart, and see whether he is conscious of cherishing love toward the people of God because they are the people of God. Does he love them because he discovers in them the amiableness of that divine religion which is altogether lovely? Does he love them not merely because they love him, or have bestowed favors upon him, not because they are of his party, but because they bear the image of his heavenly Father? Is his love active? Is it a principle that lives, that manifests itself by all those methods whereby the good of the brotherhood may be advanced? Does it discover itself in the delight that he takes in the company and conversation of the Lord's people, and in every opportunity that he has to exchange the tokens and strengthen the bonds of mutual affection? Can he from the heart adopt the resolution of Ruth, "Whither thou goest, I will go; and where thou lodgest, I will lodge; thy people shall be my people, and thy God my God."

Tell me, reader, do you feel toward the children of God as toward the children of one common Father, and the brethren of one common family? Do you love them because they bear the image of the common Father? And do you love them in proportion to the degree in which they bear the image? Can you bear and forbear with them? Can you forget their infirmities, or do you rejoice to magnify them? Can you cast the mantle of charity over their sins, and pray for them, and watch over them, and pity, and blame, and love them still? And can you feel thus, and act thus, toward the poorest and most despised of the flock, and that because he is a Christian? If so, here is your encouragement: "He that loveth is born of God." Yours is the spirit of a better world. The paradise you lost by Adam, you shall regain by Christ. Allied to spirits born on high, you shall ascend to purer regions and breathe a purer air. Far from the tumult of this apostate earth, you shall yet rest beneath the peaceful shades of Eden, where blooms immortal amaranth "fast by the tree of life."

13

Nonconformity to the World

Saints are expectants of glory. They are born from above, and have no home beneath their native skies. Here they are strangers and pilgrims, and plainly declare that they seek a better country. It is their avowed profession that their happiness and hopes are neither in nor from the present world. Their treasure is in heaven. Much as they are influenced by the spirit, governed by the maxims, awed by the frowns, and seduced by the flattery of the world, they are so far aloof from all its corrupting influence that between them and the world there is a distinct line of demarcation. Perfectly aloof from the corruptions of the world, they are not in the present life. But they are sufficiently so to make their nonconformity a distinguishing trait in their character. They have come out and are separate. They are on the Lord's side. They are a city set on a hill, raised so far above the common level of the world that they cannot be hidden. They are not of this world, even as Christ was not of this world. Such is the excellence of their character and the purity of their conduct that the world is constrained to take knowledge of them that they have been with Jesus.

The spirit of the world is incompatible with the spirit of the gospel. It is the spirit of pride and not of humility, of self-indulgence rather than of self-denial. Riches, honors, and pleasure form the grand object of pursuit with the men of the world. Worldly men are solicitous to lay up treasures for themselves, and are not rich toward God. Their great inquiry is,

"Who will show us any good? What shall we eat, what shall we drink, or wherewithal shall we be clothed?" They are sensual, not having the Spirit. Regardless of everything but that which is calculated to gratify a carnal mind, they lift up their souls unto vanity and pant after the dust of the earth. Their thoughts and their affections are chained down to the things of time and sense. In these they seem to be irrecoverably immersed. They seldom think but they think of the world; they seldom converse but they converse of the world. The world is the cause of their perplexity and the source of their enjoyment. The lust of the flesh, the lust of the eye, and the pride of life close every avenue of the soul to the exclusion of every holy desire (I almost said, every serious reflection).

This spirit, the Christian has mortified. "Now we," said the apostle, "have not received the spirit of the world, but the spirit which is of God." The heavenly mind looks down on the things of the world as lying vanities that cannot profit. The disciple of Jesus, as he has nobler affections than the worldling, has a higher object and more elevated joys. What things were gain to him, those he counts loss for Christ, yea, doubtless he counts all things but loss for the excellency of the knowledge of Christ Jesus his Lord; for whom he is ready to suffer the loss of all things, and to count them but dung that he may win Christ. While the wise man glories in his wisdom, while the mighty man glories in his might, and the rich man glories in his riches, it is his privilege to glory in the Lord; to glory in nothing save in the cross of our Lord Jesus Christ, by whom the world is crucified to him and he to the world. The character and cause of the Blessed Redeemer lie so near his heart that, in comparison with these, everything else vanishes to nothing. He views the world by the eye of faith. He sees it in a light that reflects its intrinsic importance: the light of Eternity. There, the world shrinks to a point. The fashion of it passes away. All flesh is grass, and all the goodliness thereof is as the flower of the field. Compared with durable riches and righteousness, its highest enjoyments are trifles, light as air. "Vanity of vanities," said the Preacher, "vanity of vanities; all is vanity."

As the spirit of the world is not the spirit of God's people, so the men of the world are not their companions. The saints are a peculiar people. The church is uniformly represented as a society that is distinct from the world. "We know that we are of God," said the apostle, "and the whole world lieth in wickedness." Between the people of God and the men of the world, there is an essential difference of character. The views, the desires, and the designs of the children of God are diametrically opposite to the views, the desires, and the designs of the men of the world. The one loves what the other hates. The one pursues what the other shuns. Saints are passing on the narrow way that leads to life, sinners the broad way that leads to death. Hence there is no common bond between them. The dissimilarity of character, the diversity in the great objects of pursuit, naturally draw them asunder. If there were no other ground for the expectation, therefore, than the common principles of human nature, we might look for dissension rather than unity between the disciples of Christ and the men of the world. "How can two walk together except they be agreed? What fellowship hath light with darkness? Or what communion hath Christ with Belial?" The same principles that prompt the men of the world not to select the people of God for their familiar companions also induce the people of God to choose other companions than the men of the world. There is an irreconcilable spirit between them. The friendship of the world is enmity with God. Many as may be the mutual tokens of respect, civility, and kindness (and many there should be) between Christians and the men of the world, they are, notwithstanding, two distinct classes of men. Much as Christians esteem the men of the world as good members of civil society; much as they regard their happiness, and endeavor to advance it; much as they compassionate their depravity, and deplore their prospects; much as they are conversant with them in the ordinary calls of duty—still, they are not their chosen companions. They cannot court their friendship because they are afraid of it. Evil communications corrupt good manners. "He that walketh with wise men shall be wise; but a companion of fools shall be destroyed."

Those who have mortified the spirit, and who stand at a distance from the men of the world, are also in some good degree above its corrupting influence. The claim that, from their numbers and strength, the men of the world are apt to consider themselves as warranted to make upon the opinions and practices of God's people is habitually resisted. Though good men may be often seduced by the smiles, and awed by the frowns of the world, it is no part of their general character to conform either to its pleasure or displeasure. They act from higher motives and maintain a more consistent character than to give way to indulgencies merely for the sake of pleasing the world, or to avoid duty merely through the fear of offending it. While they regard the fear of God more than the fear of man, they will not dishonor God to please the world. And while they regard the favor of God more than the favor of man, they will not purchase the favor of man at the expense of the favor of God. A habitual regard to the will and the favor of God is an effectual security against the smiles of the world. The great object of the Christian is duty; his predominant desire is to obey God. When he can please the world consistently with these, he will do so; otherwise, it is enough for him that God commands, and enough for them that he cannot disobey.

The same spirit is also an effectual security against the frowns of the world. Real Christians cannot be more afraid of the displeasure of the world than of the displeasure of God. While they dread to offend God, they cannot tamely bow to the frowns of men. Whether it is right to hearken unto men rather than unto God, you judge! This was the spirit of the early disciples; and this will be the spirit of every disciple down to the latest period of time. So far as he manifests the spirit of Christ, wherever he is, whatever he does, the fear of God uniformly predominates over the fear of man; and the love of God, rather than the love of the world, bears uncontrolled sway over his affections and conduct.

There would be no difficulty in pointing out the path of duty upon this general subject; but there is some in saying how far men may swerve from this path and yet be Christians. One thing is plain: Christians cannot be worldlings. They cannot be lovers of pleasures more than lovers of God. He who fixes his highest affections on wealth, honor, business, sensual pleasures, amusements, and the various pursuits of the present scene, cannot fix them supremely on God. "No man can serve two masters; for either he will hate the one and love the other, or else he will hold to the one, and despise the other. Ye cannot serve God and mammon."

Nor is the character of the vast multitude who attempt to make a compromise between God and the world better than that of the mere worldling. They are of their father the Devil, and the lusts of their father they will do. The mere fact that they are forever balancing between a life of devotion and a life of pleasure, that they design now to yield the empire to God and then to the world, decides the question against them.

We must not deny that the children of God are sometimes

guilty of awful defection from the standard of Christian character in their intercourse with the world. But after all, their prevailing feelings and conduct are not those of conformity to the world, but of habitual nonconformity. The principles of the new man are at war with the principles of the world. True believers have put off, concerning the former conversation, the old man, which is corrupt according to the deceitful lusts, and have put on the new man, which after God is created in righteousness and true holiness. "This I say then," said the apostle, "walk in the Spirit, and ye *shall not* fulfill the lusts of the flesh." We cannot walk after the flesh while we walk after the Spirit. While the love of God is the reigning affection of the heart, it will turn away with disgust from the allurements of the world. The spirit of Christians is a heavenly spirit. They "look not on things that are seen, but on those that are unseen, for the things that are seen are temporal, but the things that are unseen are eternal." They set their affections on things above, and not on things on the earth.

This subject presents a number of solemn questions, to everyone who is anxious to ascertain whether his heart is right in the sight of God. It is a great point with all of us to know, whether we are spiritually-minded or worldly-minded; whether we are conformed to this world, or transformed by the renewing of our minds; whether the objects of faith or of sense, things present or to come, have the predominating influence over our hearts?

What shall we say of those, and of those professing Christians too, who exhibit to themselves, and to others, all the traits of character that belong to worldly men? What of those who pursue worldly things with all that ardor, all that intemperate zeal, that enters into the pursuits of worldly men? Is there not reason to fear that they are supremely attached to earth, and are as yet aliens from the commonwealth of Israel?

What shall we say of those who love the circles of fashion more than the associations for prayer, and who court the friendship of the rich, the gay, and the honorable more than that of the humble disciple of Jesus? What of those who send forth their little ones like a flock, and their children to dance; who take the timbrel and harp, and rejoice at the sound of the organ? Was Job uncharitable when he ranked persons of this character with those who say unto God, "Depart from us, for we desire not the knowledge of Thy ways?"

What shall we say of those who are forever varying from the path of duty lest it should be unpopular, who never lisp a syllable or lift a finger for the honor of God, lest they should displease the world? What, but that they love the praise of men more than the praise of God?

Conformity to the world is to be expected from the professed worldling. It is the character of the worldling. But is it to be expected from the professed disciple of Jesus? Is it the result of the habitual determinations of a heavenly mind? Is it the character of one who looks on things that are unseen and eternal; of a stranger and sojourner; of one who sets his affections on things above, and not on things on the earth? How many, like the young man in the gospel, exhibit a decent and regular outward profession, who are wholly devoted to the world! Here their affections center. From this polluted fountain all their joys flow. They would have been Christians but for the world. But the world is the fatal snare. They have plunged down the precipice, and drifted almost beyond the hope of recovery.

If any man loves the world, the love of the Father is not in him. The expression of the apostle is not too strong: "To be carnally minded is death." Show me the men who imbibe the spirit of the world; who choose the company of the world; who imitate the example of the world; conform to the maxims of the world; are swallowed up in the gaiety, fashions, and amusements of the world—behold these are the ungodly, who are brought into desolation as in a moment! "I have seen the wicked in great power, and spreading himself like a green bay tree. Yet he passed away, and, lo, he was not; yea, I sought him, but he could not be found. Surely, Thou didst set them in slippery places; Thou castest them down into destruction."

14
Growth in Grace

How beautiful is the light of the morning! Behold it hovering over the distant edge of the horizon and shedding its cheerful beams upon the hills. It is a morning without clouds. But how soon is the prospect overcast! The atmosphere is obscured by vapors, and the sun is darkened by a cloud. Again the mists are fled; the clouds have passed over; and the sun is still advancing in his course. Thus he rises, now, behind the cloud, now, in all the greatness of his strength, shining brighter and brighter unto the perfect day. Such is the path of the just. In the present world, good men are very imperfect. The best of men have reason to complain bitterly of the body of sin and death; and the best of men too have the most ardent desires that the body of sin and death may be crucified with Christ. The highest point of Christian experience is to press forward. It is a distinguishing trait in the character of every good man that he grows in grace.

There are various similitudes used by the inspired writers that are significantly expressive of the advancement of Christians in knowledge and in piety. The young convert is likened unto one who is newly born. There is a point of time in which he begins to live. At first, he is a babe, then a child, till he finally attains unto the measure of the stature of the fullness of Christ. The kingdom of heaven is also compared to seed that is cast into the ground. First comes up the tender blade, then the thriving stalk, then the ear, after that the full corn in the ear, ripening for the harvest, and preparing for the garner of the husbandman. It is also compared to a well of water, springing up into everlasting life. No imagery in nature can more fully illustrate the growth of grace in the heart. "The righteous," said Job, "shall hold on his way, and he that hath clean hands shall wax stronger and stronger." This is the prominent feature in the character of the good man: he shall hold on his way. "The youth," said the evangelical prophet, "shall faint and be weary, and the young men shall utterly fall; but they that wait upon the Lord shall renew their strength; they shall mount up with wings as eagles, they shall run and not be weary, and they shall walk and not faint." With inimitable beauty is the good man described by the Psalmist: "And he shall be like a tree planted by the rivers of water that bringeth forth his fruit in his season; his leaf also shall not wither, and whatsoever he doth shall prosper." Grace in the heart as certainly improves and advances as a tree thrives in a kindly and well-watered soil. It flourishes in immortal youth, and blooms forever in unfading beauty.

The certainty of the believer's progress, however, rests on a surer foundation than either the degree or the nature of his religion. "We are not sufficient," said the apostle, "to think anything as of ourselves, but our sufficiency is of God." That the people of God will grow in the divine life till they reach the stature of perfect men, and are meet for the inheritance of the saints in light, is beyond all controversy. But the reason, and the sole reason, of this is that it is God who works in them to will and to do of His good pleasure. Covenanted grace is the support of the believer through every step of his pilgrimage. There is nothing in the nature of holiness that is incapable of corruption. Adam fell; angels fell; and such is the awful depravity of the human heart that, left to himself, the holiest saint on earth would draw back unto perdition. Still he shall progress in holiness throughout interminable ages. It is the economy of divine grace where God has begun a good work to carry it on, where He has given one holy exercise of heart, to give another and another, until the subject is ripened for glory.

The hypocrite, once he imagines himself to be a Christian, views his work as done. He is satisfied. He is rich, and increased in goods. But it is otherwise with the true Christian. Conversion is but his first step. His work is all before him. His graces are increasingly constant and increasingly vigorous. The more he loves God, the more he desires to love Him. The more he knows of His character, the more he contemplates the manifestations of His glory with rising delight. "As the hart panteth after the water-brooks," so his soul pants after God. Having once tasted that the Lord is gracious is not enough to satisfy him. He will ever remain unsatisfied till he reaches the fountainhead, and drinks to the full of the river of life that flows from the throne of God and the Lamb. The more he sees of the evil of sin, the more he desires to see. The more he hates it, the more he desires to hate it. The more he sees of himself, the more he abhors himself, and the more he desires to abhor himself. The more he is emptied of himself, the more he desires to be emptied of himself, the more he desires to become poor in spirit, to feel that he is cut off from every hope and to rest on Christ alone. The more he is engaged in duty, the more delight he finds in performing it. The more severe his conflict with the enemy, the harder he presses it, and the more vigorous his resolution is to maintain it to the last.

There are some things in which the increase of grace is more visible, both to the world and the subject, than others. Particularly have the people of God less and less confidence in themselves. They cherish an increasing sense of their dependence. They have been so often disappointed in their false confidences that they have in some good measure become weaned from them. They know, by bitter experience, the folly of trusting in themselves. They have learned that the way of man is not in himself, that it is not in man who walks to direct his steps. The independent, self-sufficient spirit of the carnal heart is broken down. They walk by faith and not by sight. They daily taste the sweetness of that heavenly precept: "In all thy ways acknowledge God, and He shall direct thy paths. Cast all your care on the Lord, for He careth for you."

They are more and more patient in sufferings. The more they are accustomed to the yoke, the less they repine under the weight of it.

They are also more and more charitable in their opinions of others. Young Christians are too often very uncharitable and censorious. They are more apt to take notice of the infirmities of their brethren than their graces, and the infirmities of others than their own. But the more they know of themselves, the more reason they see to exercise charity toward others. They fear to judge, lest they themselves should be also judged. They walk with all lowliness and meekness, with long-suffering, forbearing one another in love.

They have also the more full government of their passions. They are slow to wrath.

They are more and more punctual in the performance of the relative duties. Young Christians are apt to neglect them. They suffer the duties they owe immediately to God to swallow up those that belong to their neighbor. But as they advance in the divine life, they become more uniform in the exercise of grace, and more punctual in the discharge of all duty. They do not love God less, but they love their fellow men more. As they grow more fervent and more constant in their devotional exercises, so they become more circumspect, and unexceptionable in their intercourse with the world.

Perhaps there is no one point in which growth in grace is more visible than in that harmony and consistency of character that are too often wanting in young Christians, but that shine with so much beauty in those who are advanced in the Christian course.

In everything that belongs to the excellence of real religion, the true believer is in a state of progression. He seeks and strives; he wrestles and fights. He is ever aiming at the prize. View him in the early part of the divine life, follow him through the various stages of his progress, and you will find that, notwithstanding all his doubts and declensions, he makes a gradual advance. He does not feel, he does not act as though he had already attained, either were already perfect; but he follows after, if he may apprehend that for which also he is apprehended of Christ Jesus.

"This *one thing* I do," said Paul, "forgetting the things that are behind, and reaching forth to those that are before, I press toward the mark of the prize of the high calling of God in Christ Jesus." Where is the Christian who does not make the spirit of the apostle his own? Tell me, you who have just begun the heavenly race; tell me, you who are verging toward the goal; was there ever a Christian who felt satisfied with present attainments? Is not the unvarying voice, both of early and long-tried piety, responsive to the language of Paul? Yes, reader, it is both the highest point of Christian experience, and the clearest evidence of Christian character, to press forward. The disciple of Jesus desires to be perfect, to be more and more conformed to the image of Christ. He presses after this. It is his grand inquiry how to be, and how to live, more like a child of God.

Mark the way of the upright. As you trace his steps through this dreary pilgrimage, sometimes he wanders from the path;

sometimes he halts and tires. His progress is far from being uniformly rapid, and often far from being perceptible, either by himself or others. Sometimes his motion is retrograde. There are seasons when, instead of advancing, he is the subject of great defection. Still it is true that on the whole he advances. If you compare his present state and character with what they were a considerable length of time past, you will find that he has made gradual progress. I know there are seasons—dark and gloomy seasons, seasons of guilt and declension—when the real Christian will make this comparison at the expense of his hopes. Be it so. Seasons of guilt and declension ought to be seasons of darkness. I know too that there are seasons when he is liable to discouragement because he does not always experience that light and joy that crowned the day of his espousals. This is a serious error. There is a glow of affection, a flush of joy, that is felt by the young convert as he is just ushered into the world of grace, that perhaps may not be felt at any future period of his life. And you cannot from this draw the inference that he has made no advance. All this may be true, while there is a power of feeling, a strength of affection, in the saint who has passed through the wilderness and knows the trials of the way, to which the young convert is a stranger. As he ascends the mount, his eye is fixed; his step is more vigorous, and his path brighter and brighter. He remembers his devious steps, and how he traced them back with tears. But the trials of the way are forgotten. He is rising to that brightness of purity that sheds the luster of eternity on his character, and aiming at "the crown of righteousness which fadeth not away."

Here then is another test of the genuineness of your religion. I am aware that it is a severe one. But it is one that bears the seal of truth; and we must not shrink from it. Professing Christians are apt to place too much confidence on their past experience, and think little of the present; to think much on what they imagine to have been their conversion, their first work, and then give up the business of self-examination, and allow themselves to droop and decline. But the question is, what is your present character? Grace is the evidence of grace. I know it is true that he who is once a Christian is always a Christian; but it is also true that he who is not now a Christian never was a Christian. Examine yourself, therefore, and see whether you are in the faith. The best evidence in the world that you are is that you grow in grace.

Now apply the principle. Have you, on the whole, since you first began to hope that you were united to the Lord Jesus Christ, been growing in grace? The question is plain and decisive.

Do you never hunger and thirst after righteousness? Do you never see the seasons when you are conscious of the most sensible desires after increasing conformity to God?

Do you never feel the burden of remaining corruption, and ardently desire to be delivered from its power? Do you never find your heart drawn out in fervent supplication for sanctifying grace as well as pardoning mercy?

Do you now desire to press forward, to renounce everything, and to take God for all your portion? Do you strive to live nearer to Him, and are you resolved to persevere to the end in a life of faith in Him who loved you and gave Himself for you?

If you can ingenuously answer these questions in the affirmative, you are not destitute of evidence that you have passed from death unto life. But if you know nothing of all this, cast away your vain confidence. No man living in spiritual sloth, and making no new advances, ought to flatter himself that he is interested in the blessings of the great salvation. The man who is satisfied because he thinks he is safe, who feels that he has religion enough because he thinks he has enough to save him from hell, is as ignorant of the power as he is a stranger to the consolation of the gospel of Jesus Christ.

15

Practical Obedience

You have no right to call Me, "Lord, Lord," said the Savior, unless you do the things that I say. "If ye keep My commandments, ye shall abide in My love, even as I have kept my Father's commandments, and abide in His love." It is as if He were saying, "You cannot claim the character, you cannot share the privileges of My people, without yielding a cordial, a habitual, and a persevering obedience to the divine commandments."

After all that can be said of the nature of the Christian graces, after every effort to discriminate between true religion and false, the spirit of obedience to the divine commands is the grand test of the genuineness of our faith. "By their fruits ye shall know them." The plain and decisive question that should be often pressed upon the reader's conscience is this: Is the spirit of the gospel expressed in my habitual deportment?

There is a wide difference between that obedience which the gospel requires, and that which is practiced by the most advanced Christian who ever lived[*]. That obedience which,

---

[*] I am aware of the efforts that have been made, and are still being made in one form or another, both by the wise and the unwise, to pervert, if not to destroy, the moral law. Some tell us that it is abated; others say that it is not binding since the apostasy; and others say that it is not binding till after the gospel is embraced. Sometimes we are consoled with the notion that "God does not require perfect obedience of His people in this fallen state!" At other times we are quieted in our rebellion by the argument that "the

131

through the grace of God the believer is enabled to attain in the present life, and which may be viewed as conclusive evidence of Christian character, is, in the first place, cordial. It flows from the heart. "God be thanked," said the apostle to the Romans, "that ye were the servants of sin, but ye have obeyed *from the heart* that form of doctrine which was delivered you." Evangelical obedience expresses not merely the form, but the power of godliness. Everything short of that obedience that proceeds from the heart is disobedience. God neither requires nor will accept of obedience that does not spontaneously flow from supreme love to Himself. The moral quality of all actions lies in the disposition of heart with which they are performed. Actions that are apparently good may flow from a very bad heart, and, in the sight of God, are as corrupt as the heart from which they flow.

We read of those who followed our Lord with great zeal for a time, but who at length went back and walked no more with Him. And what was the reason? The love of God was not in them. Their hearts, like that of the young man in the gospel, did not enter into the spirit of the duties that they practiced. They did not love the duties themselves, nor desire to glorify God in

---

commandment is not grievous, because it is not the rule of justification!" The truth is, the law is founded in the character of God, and the relation that all intelligent creatures bear to Him. Hence, while this character and relation remain the same, the law will remain, under all possible circumstances, immutably and everlastingly binding. That obedience to the law that the gospel requires is identified with the requisitions of the Decalogue. "Do we make void the law through faith? Yea, we establish the law." Is the law so unholy that it requires abatement? Is the commandment so unjust that it could not righteously have been the rule of justification? Is God unrighteous—or is every precept of His law, under all the sanction of eternal death, of the same binding force now that it was when first proclaimed from the sacred hill?

them. Men often practice the duties of piety from some mercenary end. False motives entwine themselves into all the external duties of the hypocrite. It is not so with the obedience of the true Christian. That is deep and thorough. It proceeds from the inmost soul. There is a purity of design in all. "This is the love of God, that we keep His commandments; and His commandments *are not grievous.*" It is no task to the Christian to obey the commandments of God. It is his highest pleasure. He delights in being devoted to the service of a Being whom he supremely loves. It is his meat and his drink to do the will of Him who sent him, and to finish His work. It is with heartfelt pleasure that he consecrates his time, his talents, and his privileges to the delightful work of glorifying God. The glory of God is the great end of his being. The honor of His name is a motive, paramount to every other principle; the precepts of His law a guide, paramount to every other rule of duty. The love of Christ constrains him. When he contemplates his duty, he feels the spirit of holy enterprise; when he looks at the work that God has given him to do, he is animated with pious zeal, and is constrained to exclaim, "I delight to do Thy will, O God, yea, Thy law is within my heart!" He, therefore, who obeys God at all, obeys Him from the heart. He obeys internally as well as externally. His is cordial obedience.

But the obedience of God's people is also habitual. There are some passages of Scripture that at first view appear to inculcate the idea that the obedience of the new man is universal. Caleb and Joshua are said to have *wholly* followed the Lord. Job is called a *perfect* and upright man. Zacharias and Anna are said to have been righteous before God, walking in *all* the commandments and ordinances of the Lord *blameless.* "Whosoever abideth in Christ," said John, "sinneth not." And again, "Whosoever is born of God *doth not commit sin;* for His seed remaineth in him, and he *cannot sin* because he is born of God." And thus our Savior said, "Then are ye My friends, if ye do *whatsoever* I command you."

But if we would make the Bible consistent with itself, we must give these passages some latitude of meaning. The experience of the world and the declarations of eternal truth assure us that there is not a just man upon earth who does not sin. We must not root out all religion from the earth because we do not find perfection in men. Moses sinned, Samuel sinned, Paul sinned, Peter sinned, and yet they were all fervently pious. The melancholy fact is that the best of men sin greatly. They are sometimes the subjects of the most awful defection.

It is needless to conceal the truth that the sins of good men are of an aggravated character. It is in vain to say that they do not sin knowingly. They are indeed often surprised into the commission of sin; but they often commit it with calmness and deliberation. They often commit it in defiance to the sober dictates of reason, and in defiance to the most powerful conviction of their consciences.

It is in vain to say that they do not sin voluntarily. No man was ever constrained to sin. Sin cannot be forced upon men contrary to their own inclination. The children of God often complain that their hearts prompt them to sin, but their hearts never constrain them to act contrary to their choice. Seriously considered, it is impossible to sin without acting voluntarily. The divine law requires nothing but voluntary obedience, and forbids nothing but voluntary disobedience. As men cannot sin without acting, nor act without choosing to act, so they must act voluntarily in sinning.

The children of God therefore do sin; they sin knowingly; they sin voluntarily—but they do not sin habitually. It is not the prevailing habit of their lives to disobey the commandments of

God. This cannot be. Sin does not *reign* in their mortal bodies, that they should obey it in the lusts thereof. Between the old man and the new, there is an unceasing conflict. "The flesh lusteth against the Spirit, and the Spirit against the flesh; and these are contrary the one to the other, so that they cannot do the things that they would." Still, in the newborn soul, the flesh has not the ascendancy. The old man is crucified with Christ that the body of sin might be destroyed, that henceforth we should not serve sin. This is most surely true of every believer. It is the prevailing habit of his life to obey the commands of God. He is solicitous to perform whatever God requires, and watchful to avoid whatever He forbids. No true Christian can be habitually more engaged in the service of the world and of sin than in the service of God. His obedience, though not perfect, is habitual.

It may also be added that the conformity to the precepts of God's Word upon which we may safely rely as a test of character is persevering. The disciple of Jesus Christ perseveres in his course to the end of life. He holds on his way. It is the characteristic, as well as the blessedness of those who trust in the Lord, that they are as Mount Zion, that cannot be removed, but abide forever.

The Apostle John speaks of a class of professing Christians that were somewhat multiplied even in those early days of the Christian Church. He says, "They went out from us, but they were not of us; for if they had been of us, they would no doubt have continued with us; but they went out that they might be made manifest that they were not all of us." The true disciple endures to the end. Though he foresees that his path is beset with obstructions on every side, still he goes forward. Though dangers may threaten, and trials discourage him, leaning upon the Beloved he goes forward. His most vigorous resolutions terminate upon his duty. He goes forward with a firm and vigorous step. No matter how rough the way, with an eye fixed on the Author and Finisher of his faith, he goes forward with unabated ardor, leaving the earth behind him, and animated with the prospect of heaven and glory before him. He is aiming at the prize of the high calling of God in Christ Jesus. No difficulties are so great, no fatigue so severe, as to divert him from his design. Perfection is his object. He cherishes no present intention to disobey at all. From the heart, he desires and intends to yield a compliance, not merely to this or that requisition, but to all the divine requirements, without distinction and without exception.

We have the highest warrant to believe that obedience this cordial, habitual, and persevering is conclusive evidence of our good estate. There are none but real Christians who thus persevere in the sincere and habitual practice of godliness. "The ways of the Lord are right, and the just shall walk in them, but the transgressors shall fall therein." The way of the Lord is a highway; it is called the way of holiness, and the unclean shall not pass over it.

The Scriptures uniformly represent a life of practical godliness as a decisive test of Christian character. A holy life is the grand mark of distinction between the children of God and the children of the devil. "In this the children of God are manifest, and the children of the devil: Whosoever doth not righteousness is not of God." "Little children," said the same apostle, "let no man deceive you, he that doth righteousness is righteous; he that committeth sin is of the devil." And again, "Hereby do we know that we know Him, if we keep His commandments."

It is difficult to conceive how it can be otherwise. There is an inseparable connection between a holy heart and a holy life.

A holy life can no more proceed from an unholy heart than a pure stream can flow from an impure fountain. Wherever we find cordial, habitual, persevering obedience to the divine commands, there we have reason to believe that the love of God dwells in the heart. Show me a man who makes the law of God the rule, and the glory of God the end of his conduct, who is habitually devoted to the duties of piety and charity, and I will show you one whose heart has been sanctified by the Spirit of grace. On the other hand, show me a man who, in the general course of his life, pays no regard either to the divine law or the divine glory, who neither denies himself nor exerts himself for the honor of God and the good of his fellow men, and I will show you a man who, notwithstanding all his hopes and his professions, has never felt the power nor tasted the sweetness of genuine religion. The truth is, men sincerely and habitually act as they love to act. In forming a judgment concerning our own character, we have no right to view our practice better than our principles, nor our principles better than our practice.

At the future Judgment, there will be a public trial of human character. The grand question then to be decided will be, "Are you a child of God? Are you a believer in the Lord Jesus Christ?" This question will be decided by evidence. And the evidence that the Righteous Judge will view as conclusive will be a life of practical godliness. The Father, without respect of persons, will judge "according to every man's work." When John, in the vision of Patmos, saw the sea give up the dead who were in it, and death and hell give up the dead who were in them, they were judged every man *according to his work*. In looking forward to the process of that day, the reader may anticipate this grand rule of trial: If he leads a life of evangelical obedience, though that obedience is not the ground of his acceptance, it is evidence that he is accepted. And this is evidence that comes without looking for it. A life of humble, holy, Christ-like obedience carries hope, and faith, and comfort along with it. It is conclusive evidence that the love of Christ constrains you, and is not long maintained without filling the heart with light and joy.

Come, then, and try your heart by the same rule whereby God tries it. God has given, or He will give you, a fair opportunity of proving your religion by bringing it into action. He proved Abraham, and the trial issued in the clearest evidence of Abraham's religion. He proved the young man in the gospel, and the result of the trial was that he loved the world more than God. What is the issue of the trial in your case? Frames, experiences, professions, and hopes are nothing without lives of practical godliness. "He that hath My commandments and keepeth them, he it is that loveth Me."

The plain question that was stated at the beginning of this essay is a very important one: Does your religion express itself in your habitual deportment—in prosperity, in adversity, in the family, in the world, among friends and foes? Remember, he who has the hope of the gospel purifies himself, even as Christ is pure. Does your love for God prompt you to a devout attendance upon all His institutions? Does it animate you with increasing attachment to His Word and His service? Does your love for man lead you to do justice and love mercy, to live in peace with all men? Does it make you the better husband or the better wife, the better parent or the better child, the better master or the better servant, the better magistrate or the better subject, the better friend or the better citizen?

The religion of Jesus Christ is not a system of empty speculations, designed to have no practical influence. It is not the offspring of wild enthusiasm that exhausts all its force in feeling, and leaves none for action. A good man out of the good treasure of the heart necessarily brings forth good things. Experience without practice is nothing; and practice without experience is no more. Experimental religion consists in the reality of the Christian graces, and in their due effect upon the life and conversation. If you are an experienced Christian, you feel the power of religion in your heart and exhibit it in your life. The life of Jesus is made manifest in some good degree in your mortal flesh. You feel and act in some measure as Christ felt and acted. You display His spirit; you imitate His example; you exhibit a firm and bold attachment to His cause.

But, reader, with all your shortcomings, with all your gross violations of duty, is such the habitual course of your life? Is yours a life of devotion, of meekness, and humility; of supreme attachment to heavenly and divine things; of self-denial, and of universal benevolence? Try your heart by your practice, and your practice by your heart. If, after candid examination, you find reason to hope that you are one of God's dear children—washed with the blood, sanctified by the Spirit, clothed with the righteousness of the well-beloved—cherish that hope as the gift of heaven. Dismiss your fears; bind yourself to be the Lord's in an everlasting covenant; think less of yourself, and more and more of the name, the cross, the glory of your Redeemer. Henceforth let your light shine. "Seek ye first the kingdom of God and His righteousness, and all things shall he added unto you." Or, in other words, serve God, and God will take care of you. Submit to His will; trust in His grace, and resign yourself into His hands, with the assurance that the Lord is well-pleased with those who hope in His mercy.

16

Conclusion

Let the reader review the preceding pages in the fear of God. The subject is of eternal importance. A mistake here is a mistake for eternity. Under a deep sense of his need of the searching influences of the Divine Spirit, let him, as he reflects upon what he has read, adopt the language of the Psalmist, "Search me, O God, and know my heart; try me, and know my thoughts; and see if there be any wicked way in me, and lead me in the way everlasting."

"He that is not with Me," said the Savior, "is against Me." There is no principle within the whole compass of morals that admits of more strict demonstration than this, that there can be but two moral characters that are essentially different. There must be necessarily in every intelligent being a conformity to the will of God, or the want of it. It is as impossible that a man should be neither right nor wrong, as it is that a portion of matter, at any given period, should be neither at rest nor in motion. It is absurd to suppose that he is neither a saint nor a sinner, neither penitent nor impenitent, neither a believer nor an unbeliever. So long as men possess any moral character, they must view themselves, and be viewed by others, either for God or against Him. In the great contest that enlists the feelings and the power of three worlds, it is impossible that there should be a neutral. One side or the other will claim every intelligent being in heaven, on earth, and in hell. And it is right they should do so. If the line should now be drawn by the invisible hand of the

Great Searcher of hearts, on the one side would be the friends of God, on the other His enemies.

Allow me then, beloved reader, before I take leave of you, plainly, solemnly, and affectionately, to ask this question: On which side do you stand? If you possess nothing more than mere visible morality, nothing more than the naked form of religion, nothing more than a speculative knowledge of the system of revealed truth, nothing more than simple conviction for sin, nothing more than a vain confidence of your own good estate, connected with some apparent zeal for the cause of God, and a few transient and spurious affections—how can you be one of the children of the Everlasting Father? If you are a stranger to love for God, to repentance for sin, to faith in the Lord Jesus Christ, to evangelical humility, and to genuine self-denial—how can you cherish the hope that you are a Christian? If you know nothing of the spirit of prayer, nothing of the love of the brotherhood, nothing of mortifying the spirit of the world, nothing of growth in grace, of cordial, habitual, persevering obedience to the divine commands—how can it be that you have been brought nigh by the blood of Christ? If these things are so, you have neither part nor lot in this matter, for your heart is not right in the sight of God.

Does this agitate you? The writer of these pages takes no pleasure in exciting needless alarm. But how can he raise the unhallowed cry, "Peace, Peace," when the Eternal God says, "There is no peace"? How can he raise the unhallowed cry, when every note of the siren song would only lull the hypocrite into a more deathlike security, and every sentence prove the blow to sink him deeper into the eternal pit? Poor, self-deceived man, who vainly imagines that you are on the way to heaven while you are on the way to hell, rather than amuse you with tame, smooth, pretty things, oh, that I could raise a voice that would make you tremble, even in the grave of trespasses and sins! Be entreated to dismiss your deceptions, to give up your delusive confidence. Do not cast the anchor of hope upon a shore so yielding that the final blast will break its hold. However hard the struggle, despair of mercy without being washed in the blood of Jesus. Do not cherish a delusion that the King of terrors will tear from your heart!

But shall I presume that all my readers are hypocrites? No, many of them, I trust, are the dear people of God. Some of them may be weak in faith, and weak in hope. Beloved Christian, I would not lisp a syllable to rob you of your confidence. Though weak and trembling, there is everything to encourage and strengthen you. It cannot discourage you to examine closely whether the foundation of your hope is firm, whether your confidence is built upon the sand or whether it rests on the Rock of Ages. Feeble Christians are called upon to mourn over their weakness. Their want of strength is their sin. Their graces may be well compared to the dimly smoking flax. They emit little that warms and enlightens. Their love is cold, their joys barren and poor. God hides his face, and they are troubled. Tossed, like Peter, upon the tempestuous sea, they have hardly faith even to cry, "Lord, save, or I perish!" Still, they may rejoice. The Angel of the everlasting covenant lives. That precious covenant itself recognizes the heart-reviving principle of redemption through the blood of Jesus, forgiveness of sins according to the riches of His grace. Well then, believer, may you rejoice, even in the midst of trembling. What, though you are bowed down under the weight of guilt; what, though poor in spirit, filled with apprehension and almost hopeless; what, though you are like the bruised reed—frailty itself still more frail, ready to fall by the gentlest breeze! "A bruised reed shall He not break, and a smoking flax shall He not quench." No, never. It shall not be broken, but supported and cherished, yea, by a hand that is omnipotent; it shall be transplanted to the garden of the Lord, and flourish in the courts of our God. The Great Head will never disregard the feeblest members of His own body.

There is a peculiar adaptedness in the character of our Lord Jesus Christ to the weakness and fears of His people. Early was He designated as one who would bear our griefs and carry our sorrows, commissioned to bind up the broken hearted, and to comfort all who mourn. The man Christ Jesus is touched with the feeling of our infirmities. He knows our frame, and remembers that we are but dust. The Shepherd of Israel will gather the lambs in His arms, and carry them in His bosom, and gently lead those that are with young. It is He who gives power to the faint; and to them who have no might, He increases strength.

O believers! That we all might learn to fasten our affections, to rivet our hopes, on the cross of Christ! Here is our comfort. We must think much, and make much of Christ. In Him, all fullness dwells. He is the Captain of your salvation. He is a fountain for your uncleanness, and a light for your way. It is He who is of God made unto His people wisdom, righteousness, sanctification, and complete redemption. No matter how great your guilt, rest on Him, and He will be increasingly precious—precious in life, precious in death, precious forever. While your life is hidden with Christ in God, however languid the throb, it shall never expire.

Come, then, lift up the hands that hang down and confirm the feeble knees. The heavens and the earth shall sooner crumble into their native nothing than the feeblest lamb of the Shepherd's fold stumble and finally fall. Loose yourself, therefore, from the bands of your neck, O captive daughter of

Zion! If you have seasons of trial, do not be alarmed; if you have moments of despondency and weakness, do not be dismayed. Fear not, you worm Jacob, for you shall thrash the mountains and beat them small. Your Redeemer is the Holy One of Israel. He will strengthen you; yea, He will help you; yea, He will uphold you by the right hand of His righteousness. Say, is it not enough? Thanks be unto God for His unspeakable gift!

I close then by beseeching the reader to devote himself unreservedly to the Lord. What! "Know ye not that ye are not your own? For ye are bought with a price; wherefore glorify God in your souls and your bodies, which are His." Render unto God the things that are God's. What higher delight, what greater privilege can you enjoy than to consecrate all that you are and all that you possess to God! Come, then, and make a voluntary surrender of everything to Him, and choose His service as your highest delight.

Henceforth let it be your greatest care to honor the Lord who has bought you. "As you have received Christ Jesus the Lord, so walk in Him, rooted and built up in Him, and established in the faith, as you have been taught, abounding therein with thanksgiving." Yes, blessed Redeemer! "Other Lords besides Thee have had dominion over us; but by Thee only will we make mention of Thy name." O Thou eternal, incarnate, God! I am Thine, doubly Thine, wholly Thine, Thine forever. Amen.

Finis

Other Titles Published by the Northampton Press

Sermons on the Lord's Supper, by Jonathan Edwards. 280 pp. Hardback

Heaven Taken by Storm, by Thomas Watson. 120 pp. Hardback

Sermons on Important Doctrines, by John Colquhoun. 240 pp. Hardback

Light and Heat: The Puritan View of the Pulpit, by Bruce Bickel 188 pp. Hardback

The Christian Father's Present to His Children, by John Angell James. 312 pp. Hardback

Saving Faith, by John Colquhoun. 296 pp. Hardback

The Christian on the Mount, by Thomas Watson. 128 pp. Hardback

Why Read the Puritans Today? by Don Kistler. 20 pp. Paperback

For more information, or to order, go to
www.northamptonpress.org